Spain

Managing Editor Chris Milsome
Editor Chester Fisher
Assistant Editor Dale Gunthorp
Design Patrick Frean
Picture Research Ed Harriman
Production Philip Hughes
Illustration John Shackell
　　　　　　　John Mousdale
　　　　　　　Tony Payne
　　　　　　　Marilyn Day
　　　　　　　Colin Rose
　　　　　　　Sally Launder
Maps Matthews and Taylor Associates
Reference section Peter Field

First published 1974
Macdonald Educational Limited
Holywell House
London, E. C. 2

© Macdonald Educational
Limited 1974

Published in the United States
by Silver Burd'ett Company,
Morristown, N.J.
1981 Printing

ISBN 0 382 06100 4
Library of Congress
Catalog Card No. 75-44868

Spain

the land and its people

Carmen Irizarry

Silver Burdett Company

Contents

Who are the Spaniards?

The origins of the Spaniards

If you lived in their midst, you would discover that the Spaniards are a mixture of races. They can be fair and blue eyed as well as dark and Mediterranean, according to the ethnic group from which they stem.

And they stem from many. The country's first settlers probably wandered north over a land bridge that linked Europe and Africa. They were called the Iberians, and may have come from as far away as Egypt. Meanwhile Nordic peoples were crossing the Pyrenees to occupy the upper reaches of the Peninsula. One tribe of hunters left striking mural paintings in the northern cave of Altamira.

Two waves of Celts were to follow. The first was overrunning the north in the ninth century B.C. while Phoenician traders were founding Cádiz on the southern Atlantic Shore. In time, both Carthaginians and Greeks settled along the Mediterranean coast of Spain.

The Romans in Spain

Rome conquered Spain in the third century B.C. and made it a thriving outpost of her Empire. But fighting Germanic tribes were soon at the door. The Visigoths, strongest of them all, now laid claim to the land and established a powerful state under their elected warrior kings.

In 711 A.D. Muslims from North Africa defeated Roderick, the last Gothic King. The Moors were to stay for seven centuries. Eventually they seized three-quarters of the Peninsula, coexisting with yet another group of settlers—the Jews—and leaving an indelible trace of the Orient on the face of Spain.

▲ A *payoza* or beehive hut in the Galician woods. They were the dwellings of primitive tribes who overran the north west.

The invasions of Spain

Germanic Tribes (400 AD)
Celts (1000 BC)
Greeks (600 BC)
Romans (200 BC)
Iberians (3000 BC)
Iberians (3000 BC)
Romans (200 BC)
Carthaginians (600 BC)
Phoenicians (1100 BC)
Moors (700 AD)

▼ Segovia's Roman acqueduct towers over the street. Though 2000 years old, it still supplies water to the city.

▲ The Alhambra, palace-fortress of Granada's Moorish kings, is one of Spain's architectural masterpieces.

Some characteristic Spanish faces

▲ Basques can be fair or dark, have strong and prominent noses.

▲ Blue eyes abound in Asturias, where Celtic and Swabian influence is strong.

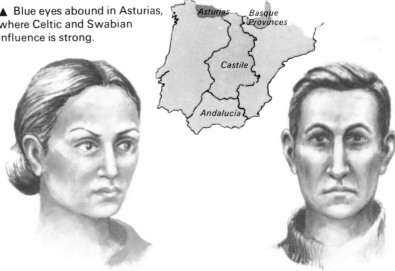

▲ Many Andalusians have olive skin and dark brown or black hair.

▲ Castilians have narrow faces and pale or sallow skins.

▲ Toledo's oldest synagogue, built in the ninth century.

▲ People from all walks of life gather to watch a popular fiesta. Spaniards have the blood of Phoenicians and Romans, Celts and Semites, Vandals and Goths.

A land of many faces

The green north

Just as racial types change from one part of Spain to the other, so does the landscape and the people's way of life.

The upper half of the country is green and rainy. Rural Galicia, its westernmost corner, was settled by the Celts, and still thrills to the sound of a bagpipe. Asturias is a land of high mountains dotted with Swiss-like chalets. In Santander and the Basque provinces, herds of plump cows graze in rolling farmland. And yet Bilbao, the Basques' largest city, is full of factories, steel foundries — and smog.

Contrasting sharply with the green north are the flatlands of Extremadura, Castile and Aragon. They run across the heart of the country, scorched by the sun in summer, bitterly cold in winter, arid twelve months of the year. Here, magnificent medieval cities — Avila, Salamanca, Segovia — rise like mirages from an expanse of ochre dust.

Ever-changing Spain

Catalonia, the other highly industrialised region, extends from the French border and has a language of its own. Its people are fiercely independent and more European than any other in Spain. Directly below their homeland lies Valencia, famous for the orange groves and vegetable gardens in its fertile Huerta.

Andalucía takes up the entire south. Its Moorish-style towns and colourful fiestas have made it famous over the centuries. Indeed, it is the only "Spain" many people know. But the tourist industry also thrives in the far-off Canaries. These volcanic islands, 60 miles off the coast of West Africa, round off the variety of landscapes and climates that make up ever-changing Spain.

There is no "one" Spain. From north to south and east to west, the climate, terrain and way of life differ sharply across the Peninsula.

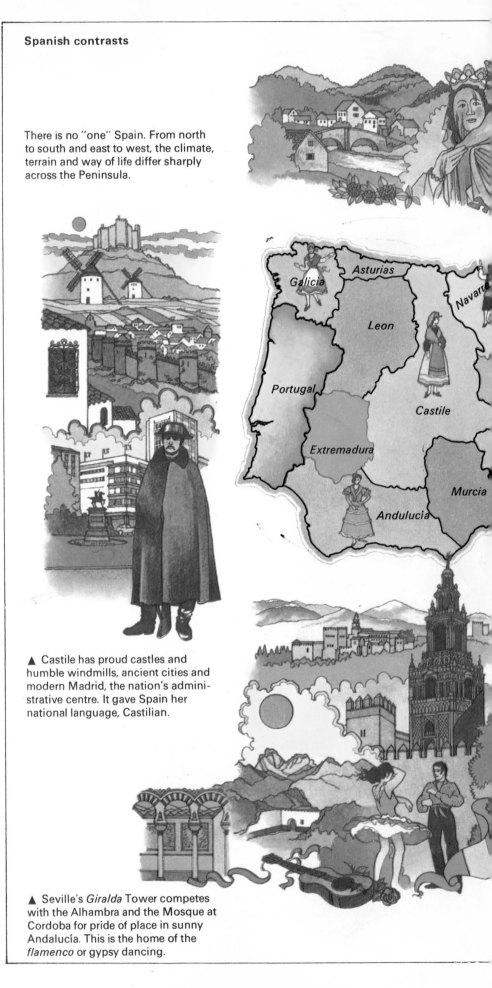

▲ Castile has proud castles and humble windmills, ancient cities and modern Madrid, the nation's administrative centre. It gave Spain her national language, Castilian.

▲ Seville's *Giralda* Tower competes with the Alhambra and the Mosque at Cordoba for pride of place in sunny Andalucía. This is the home of the *flamenco* or gypsy dancing.

◀ The north is green and rainy, a land of neat villages, pleasant meadows and snow-clad peaks. In Asturias, Roman bridges span the clear streams that tumble down from the mountains.

Catalonia

▲ Industrial Catalonia is a haven for the arts: Gaudi's Holy Family Church is a landmark of bustling Barcelona. Due south lie the orange groves of Valencia, and colourful Alicante.

▲ A refinery in Coruña, Galicia. This once-rural area, far removed from the manufacturing centres of Catalonia and the Basque country, now has its own factories and industrial complexes.

▶ Tunny fishermen haul in their nets. The sea's bountiful harvest has made fishing one of Spain's oldest and most profitable industries. Today a good portion of the catch is tinned or frozen for export.

▼ Among Spain's most forbidding landscapes are the rocky wastes of Almería. They are so similar to the American West that the province has become the headquarters for producers of cowboy films.

The Spanish influence

The Spanish Empire

With the discovery of America, Spain extended her domains far beyond the once-distant Canary Islands. Less than a century later, the King of Spain had assumed the Throne of the Holy Roman Empire, and annexed much of Europe into the bargain.

Thus, at the height of her power Spain straddled the Western World. Spanish noblemen—among them Flanders' notorious Duke of Alba—ruled the European provinces with an iron hand. Spanish dress and customs were copied all over the Continent. One of the banquet tables in the Hofburg, Vienna's Imperial Palace, is still laid "according to Spanish etiquette".

The legacy of power

In Europe, Spain's glory was shattered by uprisings, alliances between countries and shifts of power. But in America the Spanish venture prospered. For the New World was to be far more than a trading post: it became a New Spain beyond the sea. Soon thousands of settlers were sailing for what was a faithful duplicate of their homeland. The legislative system, the Church and above all the language of Spain took root in the new possessions across the Atlantic. Today, of the nearly 200 million people who speak Castilian (and Castilian is a language, not an accent), more than 160 million live in the Americas.

▼ In the sixteenth century, Spanish possessions extended from Flanders in Northern Europe to newly-discovered America. Spain's most enduring legacy to the New World was her national language, Castilian, spoken today by 160 million people.

▲ Emperor Montezuma of the Aztecs received Hernan Cortes with honours, believing him to be a god from across the sea.

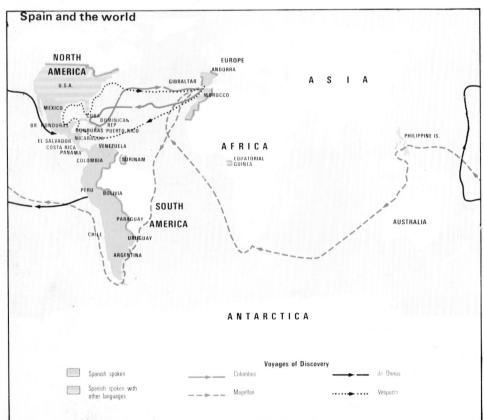

Spain and the world

NORTH AMERICA
U.S.A.
MEXICO
BR. HONDURAS
CUBA
DOMINICAN REP
HONDURAS PUERTO RICO
EL SALVADOR
NICARAGUA
COSTA RICA
PANAMA
VENEZUELA
COLOMBIA
SURINAM
PERU
BOLIVIA
PARAGUAY
SOUTH AMERICA
CHILE
URUGUAY
ARGENTINA

EUROPE
ANDORRA
GIBRALTAR
MOROCCO

ASIA

AFRICA
EQUATORIAL GUINEA

PHILIPPINE IS.

AUSTRALIA

ANTARCTICA

Spanish spoken
Spanish spoken with other languages

Voyages of Discovery
Columbus
Magellan
de Onrus
Vespucci

▲ Ferdinand Magellan, a Portuguese in the service of Spain, left Seville in 1519, groped his way down the coast of South America and discovered the Straits that bear his name. He sailed on to the Pacific and was killed in the Philippines. But Juan Sebastian Elcano completed the first voyage around the world, returning to Seville on September 8, 1522.

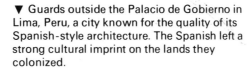

▲ Sherry is a fortified aromatic wine drunk the world over. It is named after Jerez, the Andalusian town where it is made.

▼ Guards outside the Palacio de Gobierno in Lima, Peru, a city known for the quality of its Spanish-style architecture. The Spanish left a strong cultural imprint on the lands they colonized.

Some famous Spaniards

▲ Hernán Cortes seized Mexico. Having subdued native rebellions and a rival Spanish expedition, he governed the territory for many years.

▲ The works of Diego de Silva Velázquez (1599-1660) mark a high point in European art. Court painter to Philip IV, he included his own likeness (above) in a portrait of Princess Margarita and her ladies-in-waiting called *Las Meninas*.

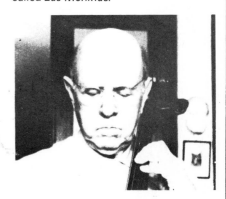

▲ Pablo Casals, Spanish humanist and musician, left his homeland after the Civil War. He was a leading cellist and one of the world's foremost interpreters of the music of Bach. He died in October 1973, aged 96.

The vital place of family life

The modern flat in Madrid where the family live.

Inside the home

All Spanish families are alike. Rich or poor, large or small, they cling together in an extraordinary manner. Grandparents, aunts, uncles and other relations take a profound interest in each other's lives. Children seldom leave home until they marry; when they do, their parents continue to regard them as a central part of the family circle.

Family life centres around a large late lunch. Father returns home from work and the children from school to have this meal which Mother has spent most of the morning putting together. If the children have lunch at school, they will join their parents for the late evening supper.

Schools close at five-thirty or six. The children then return home for their *merienda*, a substantial tea with buns, cakes or pastries. Afterwards they will go out to play until it is time for supper, called the *cena*, which is never taken before nine or nine-thirty. In many houses it is served at ten, making for a very late bedtime indeed.

The Latin tradition

Home is usually a town flat on a busy street. Spaniards, like most Latin people, like to live near shops and cafes. The automobile has made it possible for many people to move to the suburbs. Thousands of families have settled in new developments outside the large cities, where they live in detached houses with flower beds and lawns.

In July or August, the entire family will head for the mountains, the beach, or some quiet country village for the long holiday (*el veraneo*). Summer and winter, the Spanish family lives very close together.

▲ Off to the *colegio*, or school, under sister's watchful eyes—though in his case it is actually a playgroup.

▲ Father at his office. He works till late in the evening, then comes home by car.
▼ The Spanish family is very close-knit.

◄ A long, leisurely lunch is the high point of the family's day. Wine is the standard drink for adults. Children have sweetened fizzy water. But youngsters are allowed a sip of *vino* now and then.

▼ Mother spends all morning preparing an elaborate lunch. Though labour-saving devices are in common use, she devotes a good deal of time to getting the meal ready, and is especially careful to vary the menu daily.

▼ A quiet moment for Dad and the youngest child. In Spain, fathers are unusually close to toddlers and babies.

A day in the life of a Spanish family

8:00

9:00

11:00

2:00

4:00

5:00

7:00

9:30

11:00

Leisure and pleasure

▲ The balloon-seller is a permanent fixture in Spanish parks.

▼ Spanish playing cards have four suits: *oro* (gold), *espada* (swords), *copa* (goblets) and *basto* (clubs).

▲ Time for a leisurely *aperitivo* in a pavement cafe.

▲ The most popular magazines are those bought by women avid for news of the Royal Families of Europe. They outsell general-interest publications by far.

Cafes and bars

Spaniards do very little entertaining at home, but relish every chance to join friends in cafes, bars and restaurants. That is why there are so many of these eating and drinking places in their large cities. In small villages, where life is much quieter, men (and men only) will meet in small *tascas* to play dominoes or a card game called *mus*.

Tascas are bars which serve small glasses of wine known as *chatos* and aperitifs called *tapas*. Although some city *tascas* have been done up for tourists, the real ones are modest establishments with a few rustic tables set in a dim-lit room.

A few old cafes remain. Some, like Madrid's Cafe Gijón, are still the meeting places of writers and artists, but the get-togethers known as *tertulias* have vanished forever.

Late hours

Tertulias were chat clubs. Their members were people who shared the same interests and met to talk about them on a special day, at a special time. Some *tertulias* were presided over by famous philosophers and men of letters.

Today most people make for slick coffee shops called *cafeterías americanas*. No one would think of having a *tertulia* there as they are too noisy and the service too fast! Cafeterías are especially crowded in the evening, before and after the theatre and the cinema. Since films are shown at seven and eleven, some cafeterias will stay open for the late-session crowds when they emerge at one o'clock in the morning. Even at that very late hour, some Spaniards will stay for one more drink before going home.

Some famous entertainers

▲ Teresa Berganza, Spain's most famous young singer, appears in opera houses throughout the world.

▲ Nuria Espert is a leading actress who has played to delighted audiences in Spain and abroad.

▲ In costume for Madame Butterfly is soprano Victoria de los Angeles, one of the best-loved stars of the musical world.

A typical day on television

Channel 1

14.00	**News bulletins**
14.05	**First Edition** (local news)
15.35	**The Clowns** (for children)
16.00	**The Governor's Daughter** (comedy)
16.30 17.45	Off the air
18.00	Forthcoming programmes
18.05	**The House with the Clock** (children's programme)
18.25	The **chiripitiflauticos** (children's programme)
19.40	**Good Afternoon** (interviews, current affairs)
20.30	**A Swallow in Winter** (romantic serial)
21.00	**News**
21.35	**Lady Hamilton** (film)
23.45	**Late news**
00.10	Prayer and close-down

Channel 2

20.30	**Bugs Bunny**
21.00	**Roots** (long-running documentary)
21.30	**News**
22.00	**Tertulia** (discussion programme)
23.00	**Famous escapes** (adventure series)
24.00	**Last image** (epilogue)

Spanish television is run by the State. Viewing hours are short and commercials frequent. Programme schedules lean heavily on dubbed American films; news items, both local and international, are carefully edited to reflect Government opinion.

▶ The young gypsy girl is already an accomplished performer of *flamenco* dancing. The gypsies, a people of Hindu origin, arrived in Spain in the Middle Ages. This group is performing in their own cave dwelling in Grenada; others sing and dance in special night clubs known as *tablaos*.

▼ Barcelona's *Teatro del Liceo* cheers Australia's Joan Sutherland after a stirring performance. Catalans are the most music-minded of all Spaniards, have a long opera season at the *Liceo* and numerous concerts at the *Palau de la Musica*. Though expensive by Spanish standards, tickets sell out quickly.

The shopping revolution

Buying Food

In the old days the family's needs were catered for in small neighbourhood shops. Housewives exchanged gossip as they went round to the fishmonger and the butcher, the poultry man and the greengrocer. Tins were frowned upon. Everything was bought fresh, cooked and eaten on the day it was purchased.

These shops still exist. So do the large, glass-enclosed city markets with vegetable and fruit stalls, meat counters and grocers' stands. Many people still prefer markets because they have the lowest prices in town. But some of these *mercados* are being demolished to make room for modern buildings.

Nowadays there are supermarkets in all the big cities. Like their counterparts everywhere, they are clean and modern and sell everything from wine to shoe polish. But in Spain supermarkets are luxury establishments. They are for people who do not have much time to shop and do not mind paying higher prices for the food they buy.

Clothes and shoes

Clothes and household goods can be found in large department stores, and there are many boutiques with high fashion dresses and accessories. Especially attractive are the leather shops featuring wallets, handbags and cases in the classic Spanish style. Footwear also ranks high in the shopping picture. Spaniards are very shoe-conscious people and there are dozens upon dozens of *zapaterías*, as these establishments are called in all large cities and towns. Madrid has one street—Fuencarral—lined with shoe shops from one end to the other.

Shopping hours are from nine to one-thirty (or two, in the case of food shops) and four-thirty to eight. The long mid-day pause gives shopkeepers a chance to have their own leisurely lunch. From four-thirty on they will be at their jobs again, the food stores closing sometimes as late as eight-thirty. Housewives can then purchase last-minute items for the preparation of their late supper or *cena*.

Spanish money

▲ A display of shellfish, which the Spanish are uncommonly fond of. *Mariscos* are brought daily from the coast in refrigerated lorries and cooked in a variety of ways. The prices shown are pesetas per kilo (2.2 pounds).

▲ Spanish notes come in three denominations: 1,000, 500 and 100 pesetas. Coins are 50, 25, 5 and 1 peseta pieces.

▲ An outdoor vegetable stall. The produce from Valencia's *Huerta* country is of outstanding quality. It includes salad greens and root vegetables as well as fruit.

▲ A supermarket in Madrid. These self-service stores charge higher prices than smaller establishments but offer a wider choice of quality products.

▲ Weighing the merchandise in a *pescaderia*. Fish, the classical first course of a Spanish meal, can be bought in small shops like this one or at special counters in the larger super-markets. *Merluza* (a white variety) trout, sole and large sardines are all popular, as is squid —which is stewed in its own ink.

◄ A mobile sweets stall in Seville. Nougat (boxes, far left) is the king of all Spanish sweets and a special treat at Christmas. Called *turron*, it can be crunchy or soft and is made in the towns of Alicante and Jijona in the south west. Almonds and honey are amongst the ingredients in this centuries-old confection.

How things are sold

Lentils and sugar

Savouries in brine

Onions

Cheese

Eating the Spanish way

The variety of Spanish food

Whether it's time for supper or breakfast or lunch, the dishes on a Spanish menu will vary widely from one end of the country to the other. Contrary to what most people think, it's not all olive oil and garlic!

Galicians, for example, are true to their Celtic heritage even in their food: they eat meat or fish pies called *empanadas* which are first cousins to the Cornish pasty. Basques are known as the best cooks in Spain, and have excellent fish dishes. Not content with their first-rate home cooking, Basque men have "Eating Clubs" where they prepare their own special dishes and serve them to one another.

In Castile they like roast lamb and sucking pig. Valencia is the home of many famous rice dishes, among them the well-known *paella*.

It is in Andalucia that olive oil actually comes into its own; in summer it is used to prepare *gazpacho*, a cold vegetable soup which has been described as a "liquid salad".

Another delicious dish—favoured by Spaniards regardless of their province—is the potato omelette. It can be eaten hot or cold, and is always included in the picnic basket.

Desserts

Spanish desserts tend to be too sugary for most foreigners: it takes a really sweet tooth to like the egg-yolk confections known as *yemas* and the muffins called *buñuelos*. The bread sticks called *torrijas* can be delicious and satisfying. They are sugar-coated, dipped in batter, fried and eaten, alas, only during Lent.

Typical meals for a day

Breakfast: white coffee, rolls, butter, and jam or marmalade.

Mid-morning snack: Danish (called "Swiss") pastry or sandwich.

Main meal: Baked fish, stewed chicken, fruit, black coffee (espresso).

Merienda (tea): soft drinks, pastries or cake.

Aperitif: broiled mushrooms, ham, shrimp, small glass of wine.

Supper: hearty or clear soup, sautéed vegetables or meat course, fruit.

Some famous regional dishes

▲ The *paella* went forth from Valencia to become one of the most famous dishes of Spain. It is made of rice with chicken, shrimp, mussels and fish. Paella is seasoned with saffron and cooked over a low fire until the rice is perfectly done.

▲ *Pisto* is the Manchegan fare *par excellence,* and a nourishing vegetarian dish. Like its cousin the French *ratatouille,* it is made of peppers, tomatoes, onions and courgettes gently fried in oil. Beaten eggs and bits of ham can also be added for flavour.

▲ *Empanadas* are Galicia's meat and fish pies. They can be made of pork, beef or fish—big Spanish sardines are a favourite filling—mixed with onions and mild green peppers. The dish can be eaten hot or cold and is sold, ready-cooked, in many food shops.

▲ Asturias's own dish is the *fabada,* a bean, bacon and sausage stew designed, like *empanadas,* to keep people warm during the long rainy winter. *Fabada* derives its name from the *faves*—its succulent broad beans, which absorb a smoky flavour from the pork.

▲ A Galician spread with scallops, mild *ribeiro* wine, octopus, sardines, turnip greens and potatoes for the *caldo* stew, and an enormous loaf of bread.

Gambas, the Spanish prawns, are taken as aperitif with beer or wine.

Make yourself a Spanish meal

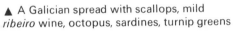

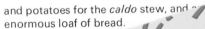

GAZPACHO

4 slices of bread (without crusts)
4 tablespoons vinegar
2 tablespoons water
1 small clove garlic
3 large ripe tomatoes
1 green pepper
½ cucumber, peeled
⅓ teacup olive oil

Mix the vinegar and the water and pour over bread. Let stand. Meantime, put the garlic, cut-up tomatoes, peppers and cucumber in blender. Add the oil, then the bread, which by now should have soaked up the vinegar. Turn on the machine and blend until ingredients are reduced to the consistency of a thick *purée*. Pour out. Add water and put in refrigerator. Or else add ice cubes and let the soup stand until they melt. Season to taste. When cold, serve garnished with bits of green pepper, onion and cucumber, and tiny cubes of bread. *Gazpacho* keeps very well in the refrigerator, either as a concentrate or diluted and ready to serve.

SACROMONTE OMELETTE

4 eggs
2 small onions
1 green pepper
½ small tin pimentos
butter or oil for frying
pinch of salt

Cut up onions and peppers and fry until soft. Add the pimentos. Mix well. Add a pinch of salt to the eggs and beat well. Then add one-third of the eggs to the mixture in the pan, lifting the sides with a spatula so that liquid covers the vegetables. Add the remaining eggs.

Wait until the egg mixture has set, that is, until the bottom is slightly toasted and the surface is still moist (not runny). Put the spatula under the omelette and detach it gently from the pan. Place a dinner plate over the pan and flip pan over so that omelette falls onto plate. Scrape away any bits of mixture stuck to the pan and add more fat if necessary. Slip omelette back into it, this time undone side down. Cook until this side has set.

BANANA FRITTERS

4 oz flour
¼ teaspoon salt
1 egg, slightly beaten
½ oz butter
6 tablespoons milk
1 egg white
1 oz sugar
3 tablespoons rum or brandy
6 ripe bananas, cut lengthwise and then into quarters
oil or fat for frying
icing sugar

First make the batter. Sift flour and salt, stir in beaten egg and melted butter. Add milk and mix well. Beat egg white till stiff and fold into batter. Mix sugar with rum or brandy and add the bananas, stirring them in the mixture until they are well coated. Let stand for about half an hour.

Drain the banana pieces on absorbent paper, dip them in the remaining flour, then in the batter. Deep fry them in oil for a few minutes until they are crisp and golden. Sprinkle with the icing sugar and serve hot.

The spread of education

Old and new education

Formal schooling was a luxury in the post-Civil War years. In those days only the children of middle and upper-class families obtained an education; the sons and daughters of workers and peasants left school at 10 or 11 to help their parents earn a living.

The Spanish educational system is now undergoing a radical reform. Every child, regardless of social standing, will remain in school between the ages of 8 and 13. This basic education leads to a three-year secondary school course from which the student emerges at 16. If he or she intends to go on to university, a further year of study is required.

The schools

The majority of middle-class children attend private schools run by the Church. There are separate institutions for boys and girls. The school buildings are usually modern and well appointed and the teachers are priests or nuns, although there may be lay assistants as well.

Uniforms are always worn in Spanish schools. The school day begins at nine or nine-thirty with a break for lunch at one. Classes resume at four-thirty and go on until about six.

In the past Saturday was a compulsory half-day. Now most schools have adopted the *semana inglesa* (or English week) which gives pupils a free weekend.

▲ Sprinting across the playing field. Athletics were once snubbed in favour of book learning. They are now emphasized in primary and secondary schools. Television campaigns also urge adults to take up sports.

◄ The playground of the *Instituto Ramiro de Maetzu*, one of Madrid's most modern secondary schools. It is government-sponsored, offers scholarships to bright children and evening classes for those who have had to leave school and wish to return to their studies.

▼ A maths lesson. The discipline is strict and academic standards are high. Many classrooms in Spain, like this one, display a crucifix and a photograph of Generalisimo Franco.

The new education system

Secondary school is for children from 14 to 16.

Primary education begins at age 6, is compulsory to age 13.

Students seeking further education take one-year **pre-university course.**

Trade school courses are offered for future technicians after age 16.

Qualified applicants gain admission to the nation's **universities.**

Candidates for science and engineering degrees attend **higher trade school.**

◀ A religious teacher and his class in Viella. In this small town high in the Lérida Pyrenees, the boys wear smocks over their clothes instead of uniforms.

▼ A hot lunch for children who do not go nome at noon. Most of them will try to join their parents for the large midday meal. If they cannot, the school will offer a good substitute.

▲ Stern-faced university students look through the daily papers. Their demonstrations for freedom of speech and assembly have been disrupting Spanish life for several years. They take the form of sit-ins and protest marches, resulting in violence and the closing down of colleges.

Faith and ritual

▲ A woman deep in prayer at a village shrine.

▼ Penitents in a Holy Week procession. They march alongside the *pasos* or sculptures that are borne through the streets. Some penitents carry heavy crosses, others drag chains fastened to their ankles.

The roots of religion

Whether he is personally devout or not, religion is an integral part of a Spaniard's life. He is almost always baptized a Catholic. Thereafter, the milestones of his life are marked by religious rites: the First Communion which initiates him into the Church, the marriage ceremony performed by a priest, the funeral Mass before he is buried in consecrated ground.

The roots of religion in Spain go deep. For centuries the Faith was at the heart of the nation's politics and, more happily, of its art. Painters like El Greco and Zurbarán brought new glory to religious themes. The great mystic, Saint John of the Cross, gave the world some of its finest religious poetry.

Triunfalismo

But if these masterpieces of Catholic art enriched men everywhere, on the national level the Faith bred a special kind of arrogance. Its critics call it *triunfalismo*, or aggressive piety. Over the centuries, *triunfalismo* repressed all non-Catholic beliefs while fostering spectacular rituals for the masses. The Holy Week processions, still staged today, are among the most dramatic religious demonstrations in the world.

Catholics of the new generation, including many young priests, oppose *triunfalismo* and think religion should be a personal encounter with God, as John of the Cross himself practised it. Their beliefs stem from the Second Vatican Council, a worldwide assembly of Catholics held in 1965. The Council brought religious liberty to Spain and gave her Church a more modern, tolerant outlook. But Reform Catholics are a minority in a country where religion is still a ritual, and pageantry its principal expression.

▶ Santiago, patron saint of Spain. The name derives from Sant-Iago, this being an early form of "James". His shrine in Compostela was thronged with European pilgrims in the Middle Ages.

▼ St. Theresa of Avila, who lived in the sixteenth century, was a nun of the Carmelite Order. A highly gifted woman, her writings rank among the classics of Spanish literature. They include a remarkable autobiography.

▲ The likeness of Mary the Virgin affixed to the wall of a mercury mine in Almadén.

▼ Soldiers in attendance at the Catholic feast of Corpus Christi.

▼ Among Segovia's most beautiful buildings is the *Iglesia de la Vera Cruz,* or Church of the True Cross. It was built in the twelfth century for the Knights Templars, a military order with branches in all of Europe.

Superstitions and customs

Witches and ghosts

Galicia is the most superstitious of all Spanish regions. "I don't believe in witches", protests the typical *gallego*, adding at once: "But they do exist".

Just as the Galicians' love of ghosts is associated with the Catholic devotion to the souls in purgatory, many Spanish superstitions spring from religious roots. If something is misplaced, for example, people pray to St. Anthony, who heads the "Lost Property" office in Heaven. They hope that this kind of saint will help them find it.

Helpful saints

Another custom derives from the striking medieval practice of making a "promise" to a favourite saint in return for a special favour. Some of these promises entail the wearing of the saint's "own" colour for a specified length of time—brown for St. Francis, purple for Jesus of Medinaceti, etc. Though the superstition is dying out as times change, one can still see peasant women in plain-coloured dresses tied with cords—the "habit" of the obliging saint who heard their prayer.

Some everyday customs

▲ Hugging is a mark of affection. It is done in public even by grown men.

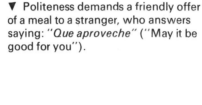

▼ Politeness demands a friendly offer of a meal to a stranger, who answers saying: *"Que aproveche"* ("May it be good for you").

▲ Children stay up for the nine-thirty or ten o'clock supper. Sometimes they will even play for a while afterwards before going off to bed.

▼ The mother is the central figure in the Spanish family. She wields enormous influence over her children, even after they have married and left home.

Spanish sayings

▲ "You can't rush the dawn by getting up earlier". Some things will only happen in their own good time.

▲ "Keep your mouth shut and no flies will go inside it". Be discreet and you'll never get into trouble.

▲ At the stroke of midnight on New Year's Eve, Spaniards reach for the "lucky grapes". If they want to have a year of prosperity and good fortune, they must eat twelve of them before the chimes have stopped.

◀ A pair of Granada newlyweds have rushed from the church to the killing of the bulls. Along with the crowd, they applaud the fine "job" *(faena)* being done by the unseen matador.

▲ San Fermin celebrations open in Pamplona. The dummies flanking the band are called *Gigantes y Cabezudos* ("Giants and Bigheads") and feature in many other Spanish fiestas.

◀ Each university college has its own *tuna* or students' string band. They wear medieval costumes and are much in demand for parties.

▶ The famous stampede of the bulls through the streets of Pamplona. Boys have been killed as they alternately taunt and flee from the bewildered animals. Later the beasts will be killed before large crowds.

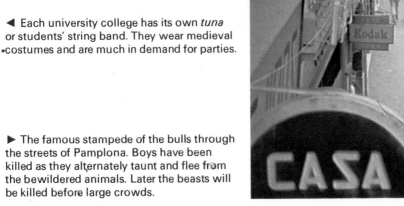

Bullfight!

▲ El Cordobés, now retired, brought a "rock-pop" look to bullfighting.

The ritual of bullfighting

A bullfight is the artistic killing of six animals before a paying audience. It is the Spanish national festivity.

Bullfights are divided into three parts. First, *picadors* taunt the bull with long poles to rouse its defensive instincts. Next comes the placing of three-centimetre barbs in the animal's neck. Meanwhile, the "killer" or *matador* is studying the beast's reactions to these "punishments" (*castigos*). He brings the show to a close by executing ballet-like steps called "passes" around the fighting animal before running it through.

The dead bull is then dragged out and another one is released into the ring.

The origins of bullfighting

Bullfighting has its earliest origins in the figure of Mithras. He was the bull-slaying god of the Persians, whose cult spread like wildfire among the legions of ancient Rome. In medieval Spain aristocrats lanced bulls from horseback (as they do even today). Eventually, the practice was taken up by men of the lower classes who killed on foot, and the modern commercial bullfight was born.

There are quite a few people in Spain who do not like bullfights. But they are considered abnormal and unpatriotic. The typical Spaniard feels nothing but indifference or repugnance before any type of life that is not human. He regards animal-bashing as good fun and, when it is made into a show, considers it a noble human endeavour and indeed a form of art.

▲ El Cordobés does a "job". This pop bullfighter won a large following for his unorthodox style which, however, put off

The stages in a bullfight

▲ At five o'clock sharp the band plays a rousing *paso doble* as the matador marches into the ring at the head of his *cuadrilla* or team of assistants. Bullfights are said to be the only events in Spain that ever start on time.

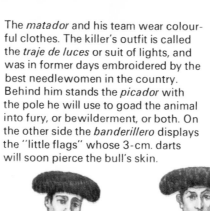

The *matador* and his team wear colourful clothes. The killer's outfit is called the *traje de luces* or suit of lights, and was in former days embroidered by the best needlewomen in the country. Behind him stands the *picador* with the pole he will use to goad the animal into fury, or bewilderment, or both. On the other side the *banderillero* displays the "little flags" whose 3-cm. darts will soon pierce the bull's skin.

Banderillero

Matador

Picador

many lovers of classical killing. A millionaire several times over, El Cordobés has a large country estate and pilots his own plane.

The matador and his team

▲ A *picador* taunts the bull with his long pole to arouse its fighting instincts. The animal has begun to battle for its life.

▲ The *faena* (literally "job"): the bull charges the matador's cape before a sword is thrust deep in its flesh.

▲ *El arrastre* or "dragging out". The dead beast is pulled from the ring by a team of mules.

A growing interest in sport

Professional soccer reigns supreme as the favourite spectator sport in Spain. On the day of a big match, hundreds of people are turned away from stadiums like the Santiago Bernabeu, home of the *Real Madrid* (capacity 100,000). Leading players rank with cinema stars; they are mobbed by fans and appear frequently in the picture magazines.

When Manuel Santana won fame for Spanish tennis on the courts of Wimbledon, the game became very popular. Now televised matches draw large and enthusiastic audiences.

Among the action sports, skiing is in the forefront. This is not surprising if one considers Spain has an abundance of mountains with deep, powdery snow—and that developers are putting up lodges and chair lifts everywhere. Each winter hundreds of young people crowd the slopes, which are beginning to attract seasoned skiers from the rest of Europe, and America as well.

Swimming, basketball, athletics and other amateur sports are becoming increasingly popular, not only as pastimes, but as aids to physical fitness.

REAL MADRID

Some triumphs of *Real Madrid*

Spanish League Champions—1961, 1962, 1963, 1964, 1965, 1967, 1968, 1969, 1972.
Spanish Cup Winners—1962, 1970.
European Cup Winners—1955-6, 1956-7, 1957-8, 1958-9, 1959-60, 1965-6.
European Champions of the Year—Alfredo Di Stefano (*Real Madrid* and Spain) 1957, 1959. Raymond Kopa, 1958.

Real Madrid has been acclaimed as the greatest club of all time. In Spain, it has dominated the league championship for many seasons, and has won the Spanish equivalent of the British Cup Final three times in recent years. The first five years of the European Cup were victories for *Real Madrid* and its strong attacking style. In addition it has had several of the great European players in its ranks, among them Di Stefano, Kopa and Puskas.

▲ Capacity crowd at the Santiago Bernabeu, *Real Madrid's* home stadium. The rival city team is the *Atlético.*

▲ Real Madrid shows its style. It is one of the world's top teams, and won the European Cup five years running.

▲ *Real Madrid* club emblem. *Real* means "Royal", a title bestowed on the team by Alfonso XIII in 1920.

▲ Fans lend noisy support to the *Real Madrid,* which they often follow to the provinces and even abroad.

How pelota is played

Basque *pelota* is played in a two-walled court called a *fronton*. The object is to hit the ball against the wall in such a way as to make it difficult for the opponent to return it. *Pelota* can be played by hand, with gloves, with a bat called a *pala*, or a wicker basket called a *cesta*. The scoring is done by agreeing to a number of points beforehand, and playing until this number is reached by either side. Pelota is one of the fastest and most strenuous games in the world. Few can play it well after the age of 30.

▲ Zoco, *Real Madrid* captain, in action in a game against *Ajax* during the European Cup Championship.

▲ Francisco Fernandez Ochoa wins the gold medal in the men's slalom at the Winter Olympics in Japan, 1972.

Cycling in Spain

Professional cycling is one of the leading spectator sports in Spain. Long-distance events such as the *Vuelta a España* and its sister competitions on the Continent draw large audiences to T.V. sets in homes, bars and cafes. The massed cyclists, called *el peloton* or the "platoon", are often filmed from helicopters, and can be seen pedalling their way up steep hills. Alongside the competitors, friends drive cars carrying spare bikes on the roof. Races go on for days. When the last lap is reached and the winner streaks over the finishing line, he is presented with a trophy, flowers, and a kiss from a pretty girl.

► Ace cyclist Luis Ocaña during the fourteenth stage of the Tour de France. His progress is followed by thousands of eager fans on television.

▲ Manuel Santana won the men's singles championship in Wimbledon. He has made tennis popular in Spain.

The Catholic monarchs

Uniting Spain

They made a handsome pair at their wedding in 1469. The groom was dark and slender. The bride was an 18 year old blue eyed blonde, as pretty as she was strong willed. He was Ferdinand of Aragon; she was Isabella, heiress of Castile.

It was a match that brought together the two most powerful Christian kingdoms of the country and marked a turning point in its history. For the combined armies of Ferdinand and Isabella were to put an end to seven centuries of warfare against the Moors. When the last Muslim king surrendered to them, Spain became a Christian nation.

Creating a powerful state

Ferdinand and Isabella ruled jointly. He turned his lively mind to foreign affairs. She set about the task of destroying the pockets of religious dissent left after the defeat of the Moors and, in 1492, decreed the expulsion of all Jews who would not convert to Christianity. The Inquisition then began to punish heretics.

That same year, Columbus discovered America and took possession of it for Spain. It was Isabella who had befriended the navigator and encouraged him to sail due west in search of the Indies. What many had thought madness proved a triumph for the cool, purposeful Queen.

Ferdinand and Isabella were the creators of the modern Spanish State. They unified the country. They brought it the wealth of the New World, on which it was to live for centuries. Above all, they set the pattern for an authoritarian form of government that has survived to this day.

▲ Columbus is received by Isabella and Ferdinand in Barcelona upon returning from his voyage of discovery. He brought back two Indians and a sample of native implements and handicrafts. He gave the king and queen a long description of the lands he had come upon. Next year (1493) Columbus set sail again. In all he made four trips to the New World.

The Spain of Ferdinand and Isabella

▲ Castile and Aragon were the largest Christian kingdoms in Spain at the time of Isabella's and Ferdinand's marriage.

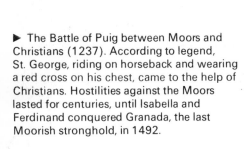

▶ The Battle of Puig between Moors and Christians (1237). According to legend, St. George, riding on horseback and wearing a red cross on his chest, came to the help of Christians. Hostilities against the Moors lasted for centuries, until Isabella and Ferdinand conquered Granada, the last Moorish stronghold, in 1492.

The power of the Inquisition

◄ The Holy Office, or Inquisition, tried and punished heretics. Some had their property confiscated and were made to do public penance; others were put to death. In this fourteenth century depiction of an *auto de fe* or public execution, Inquisition soldiers bring in three heretics. Two of them wear dunce caps and the pinafore-like penitential garment called the *sambenito*. A friar (holding crucifix) offers them absolution: those who received it were granted the "privilege" of being strangled instead of burned. On the scaffold two victims are already at the stake. Jews were the first target of the Inquisition, which shifted its attention to Protestants in the sixteenth century. Besides bringing criminal charges against heretics, the Holy Office staged book burnings. It also persecuted intellectuals suspected of having non-Catholic leanings.

Discovering a continent

▼ Columbus's flagship, the *Santa Maria*, weighed 100 tons, carried 52 men. It sailed from Palos, Huelva, on August 4, 1492. Along with it went the *Pinta* (50 tons) and the *Nina* (40 tons), both with crews of 18. All three sailed on despite bad weather and the grumbling of apprehensive sailors who came near to mutiny.

▲ After his long and harrowing voyage, Christopher Columbus sets foot on San Salvador Island on October 12, 1492. He claimed the newly discovered land for the Crown of Castile and Aragon.

▲ Portrait of the Discoverer, said to have been either Genoese or an Andalusian Jew.

Philip II
the hermit king

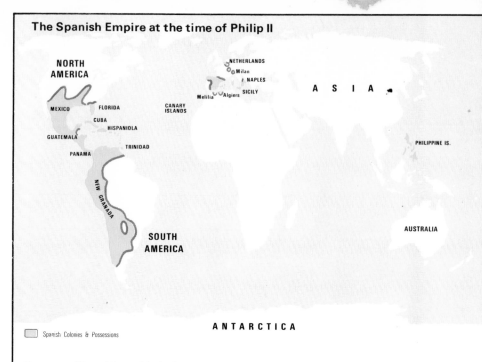

The Spanish Empire at the time of Philip II

NORTH AMERICA

MEXICO
FLORIDA
CUBA
GUATEMALA
HISPANIOLA
PANAMA
TRINIDAD
NEW GRANADA
CANARY ISLANDS

SOUTH AMERICA

NETHERLANDS
Milan
NAPLES
Melilla
Algiers
SICILY

A S I A

PHILIPPINE IS.

AUSTRALIA

ANTARCTICA

☐ Spanish Colonies & Possessions

A very serious king

Philip II delighted in paperwork and spent hours doing it in his monkish office at the Escorial. Indeed, he was the most accomplished clerk of his own realm—a pale man with the melancholy features of his Austrian forebears and the single-mindedness of his great-grandmother, Isabella.

Like her, Philip II saw Catholicism as the only possible religion. As consort to Mary Tudor, in far-away England, he had advised his wife to be lenient in her dealings with Protestants; and yet, back in Spain after her death, he moved swiftly to crush the Protestant ideas that had infiltrated the country. The leaders of what might have been the Reformed Churches of Spain died, like the Jews before them, on the Inquisition pyres.

Battles won and lost

Philip's blows for Catholicism reached far and wide. Concerned about the rising power of the Turks, he dispatched a fleet to engage their naval forces. Under the command of his half-brother, Don Juan of Austria, it won a resounding victory over the Infidels off Lepanto, Greece, in 1572.

Twelve years later Philip sent off an Armada against England, then ruled by Mary's half-sister, the Protestant Elizabeth. This time his huge fleet (which was never called "Invincible" by the Spanish) met defeat at the hands of the British.

More monkish than ever, Philip continued tending to his Kingdom and its New World colonies from his "cell" at the Escorial—a sad old man who may have known that the end of the Empire was at hand.

Bent over his writing table in Escorial, Philip controlled the affairs of his father's vast Empire, enlarged by the continuing settlement of America.

The Spanish army was feared throughout Europe. Philip acquired Portugal, but engaged in expensive and protracted warfare in the Netherlands and France.

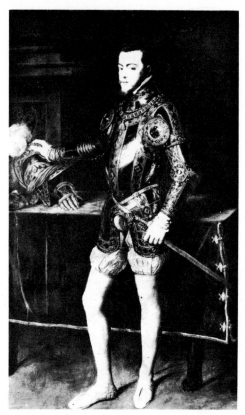

▲ Philip II as a young man, by the Italian painter Titian.

▶ In 1588 Philip's invading Armada was set upon by a British fleet under Francis Drake. Fireboats destroyed many Spanish ships in Calais harbour and a storm finished off the rest.

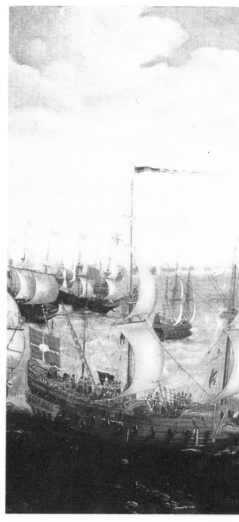

▲ Mary Tudor, daughter of Henry VIII and Catherine of Aragon, became Philip's second wife. The marriage was childless and upon Mary's death Philip returned to his country. He sought to depose her Protestant successor, Elizabeth, by sending the Armada to invade England.

▲ The library at Escorial, the great monastery built by Philip.

▲ Detail from "The Burial of Count Orgaz". This mural by El Greco, an artist of Greek birth, dates from 1586. El Greco painted himself among the gentlemen in the back (second from left).

The Civil War and Franco

A disastrous war

One of the bloodiest wars in modern history was fought in Spain between 1936 and 1939. On one side was the constituted government; on the other were the rebels who sought to overthrow it. Three European countries took a direct hand in it. Volunteers from several others, including Britain, also joined in the fighting.

After centuries of severe and authoritarian government Spain was proclaimed a republic in 1931. In an effort to redistribute the nation's wealth, the new rulers seized the estates of the landed gentry. They allowed workers to negotiate freely with their employers. They confiscated Church property and banned religious education.

These great changes in society were resisted by some and encouraged by other Spaniards. Priests thundered against the government while mobs burned church and killed priests. Wide scale violence a tit-for-tat political assassinations followed

The rise of Franco

The war began at a colonial garrison North Africa. In 1936 its officers and me led by Generalisimo Franco, rose again the government. Army units on the mai land were quick to join the revolt. Soon t troops from Morocco had crossed the Strai of Gibraltar and launched an offensive the south. Another army leader, Gener Mola, rallied more insurgents in the nor and set out with them across the Peninsu hoping to join forces with Franco's men.

The war went on for three long year Fascist Germany and Italy threw the weight behind the rebels. Communi Russia backed the Loyalists, as did th

▲ General Francisco Franco in the 1930s. He assumed command of the revolt against the Republican government.

▶ Republican refugees stream into France Many others settled in Mexico and South America. They suffered great hardships.

Los Nacionales

MINISTERIO DE PROPAGANDA

◀ A Republican poster pokes fun at Franco' backers: Germany (left), the Church, Italy (in soldier's uniform) and Morocco.

"International Brigades" made up of French, British and American Friends of the Republic.

Triumph of the rebels

From the beginning the rebels were superior in training, discipline and, with the help of Nazi Germany, in air power. Ranged behind Franco, a man of formidable military acumen, they crushed the Republic's ill-assorted, ill-equipped "*milicianos*".

When the dust settled over a devastated Spain in 1939, one million Spaniards lay dead and the country had reverted to the absolute, one-man rule of the past under a supreme Chieftain or *Caudillo*, the triumphant Generalisimo Franco. On Franco's death in 1975, King Juan Carlos assumed the Crown and the nation made ready to establish a Parliamentary democracy.

▲ Picasso's *Guernica* was inspired by the Germans' destruction of a Basque town in support of Franco. Waves of planes hit one after the other in non-stop raids—a technique which was to be perfected during the Second World War.

▲ Government militiamen fire against rebel troops under siege in Toledo's ancient Alcázar.

▲ Federico García Lorca, one of Spain's brightest young poets. He was shot by rebel sympathisers in Granada.

▲ The Valley of the Fallen, a memorial to the Civil War dead. Carved out of a mountain it houses a church and a monastery.

◄ Franco greets Juan Carlos, who assumed the Crown in 1975 on the death of Franco.

Madrid the hub of Spain

▼ Centuries ago bears were plentiful in the forests around Madrid, and the animal was enshrined in Madrid's Great Seal. The tree is a *madroño*, which gives a species of berry. Hence Madrid is known as "the city of the bear and the berry tree". It is one of three European capitals with this beast as its symbol, the others being Berlin and Berne.

Philip's capital

Madrid was a small town in Castile when it became the capital of Spain in 1561 by order of Philip II. It could not compare with Toledo, the splendid old Imperial City. But Philip liked its location at the heart of the Peninsula, on a windswept plateau overlooking the Guadarrama Mountains.

So the court moved to the town by the Manzanares—a stream so puny that courtiers dubbed it "an apprentice river". Poets and playwrights, painters and musicians made it their home. The civil servants multiplied, as did the tradesmen who arrived to serve them.

For centuries Madrid remained a quiet town whose only industry was the bowing and scraping of court life, or—after the Civil War—the shuffle of papers in government offices. Then it was caught up in the economic boom of the sixties. In ten years the staid old capital became a noisy metropolis.

Today the city is ringed with factories and full of office blocks and the motor car has transformed its once-famous air into a nasty haze.

The Coat of Arms of Madrid

▲ The Gran Via is Madrid's main artery. It is lined with shops and cinemas and crowded most of the day.

▶ In the centre of the Plaza de Espana is a monument to Cervantes. The building on the left is the Torre de Madrid, an office and flats complex.

Old and new Madrid

People hurry all the time—in and out of underground stations, buses, taxis. But the old quarter is still there, with its narrow streets, town houses and churches. Spaniards call it "the Madrid of the Austrians" because it dates from the days of the Hapsburg Monarchy. At its heart is a perfect collo-aded square called *Plaza Mayor*.

The Royal Palace stands on a bluff on the site of an old Moorish fortress. It bears a striking resemblance to Buckingham Palace, although it is not the home of a sovereign. The building is used on ceremonial occasions only by Generalísimo Franco. Prince Juan Carlos, pretender to the throne, lives in the Palacio de la Zarzuela on the outskirts of the city.

The suburbs of the capital are now a long succession of housing estates, with blocks of flats as far as the eye can see. Madrid has become an industrial and commercial centre in Spain. In the process, many of the surrounding towns have been swallowed by Greater Madrid. If this growth keeps up, the city may yet reach across the Castilian plains and swallow old Toledo.

Things to see in Madrid

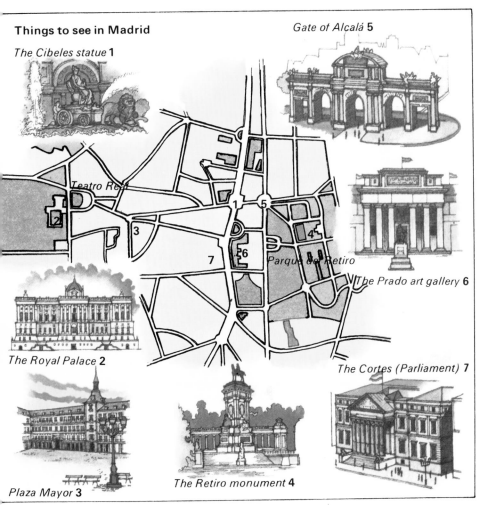

The Cibeles statue 1

Gate of Alcalá 5

Teatro Real

Parque del Retiro

The Prado art gallery 6

The Royal Palace 2

Plaza Mayor 3

The Retiro monument 4

The Cortes (Parliament) 7

▲ Dawn breaks over El Rastro, Madrid's flea market. On Sundays it is jammed with shoppers browsing among the stalls and antique shops.

▼ The Gran Via at night. Cafes and restaurants come alive around ten o'clock, and stay open until well past midnight.

Tourism
the new invasion

Cardboard Spain

In the days before the tourist boom, only a handful of travellers ventured into Spain. Now they come by the millions—in trains, planes and motor cars—to lodge in modern hotels surrounded by souvenir shops, restaurants and supermarkets.

Many people who knew Spain before the tourist invasion are unhappy about the changes it has brought about. They point to quaint villages that have been swamped by tourist shops and bars, and to high-rise hotels stretching along the coast. They feel that many tourists, content to think of the country as a few square yards of sand with a hotel room behind it, are seeing only the cardboard Spain that has little or nothing to do with the nation and its people.

But deplorable as these side-effects might be, tourism has been an important factor in breaking Spain's age old isolation and bringing her face to face with the twentieth century.

Tourist money

Furthermore, tourism has been an economic boon for Spain, providing her with foreign currency and a multitude of jobs. And the relative cheapness of Spanish holidays has enabled millions of Europeans to enjoy a holiday in the sun.

▲ Benidorm, the Mediterranean boom-town. Thousands of holidaymakers from Britain and the Continent descend upon it. In summer they are joined by crowds from Madrid who think nothing of driving the 200 miles for only a few days' stay.

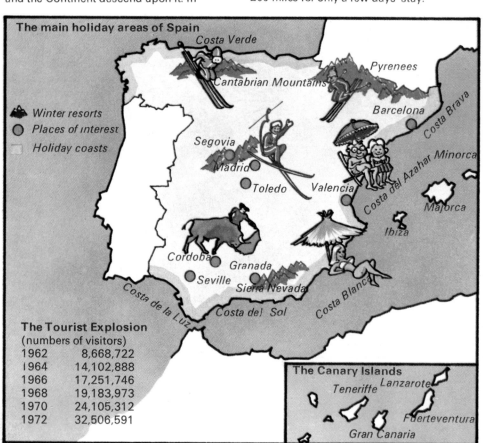

The main holiday areas of Spain

Costa Verde
Cantabrian Mountains
Pyrenees
Barcelona
Costa Brava
▲ Winter resorts
◯ Places of interest
☐ Holiday coasts
Segovia
Madrid
Toledo
Valencia
Costa del Azahar
Minorca
Majorca
Ibiza
Cordoba
Granada
Seville
Sierra Nevada
Costa de la Luz
Costa del Sol
Costa Blanca

The Canary Islands
Teneriffe
Lanzarote
Fuerteventura
Gran Canaria

The Tourist Explosion
(numbers of visitors)

Year	Visitors
1962	8,668,722
1964	14,102,888
1966	17,251,746
1968	19,183,973
1970	24,105,312
1972	32,506,591

▲ Torremolinos street scene. What was once a quiet fishing village has become a jumble of shops and bars.

A present from Spain

▲ Castanets are used to accompany most Spanish dances. They are harmoniously pitched, with lower tone on left hand than on the right.

▲ Toledo is known for its *damasquinado* or inlaid gold work, and for finely tempered swords forged from its famous steel.

▲ *Cuero repujado* is the Spanish for Moorish-inspired relief work on leather which adorns bags, hassocks and other objects.

▲ Ceramics going back to Iberian times, are one of the most colourful and unspoilt of all Spanish handicrafts.

▼ Horse-drawn carriages take visitors for a ride past Seville's *Giralda* tower. The city retains much of its southern charm and attracts many tourists.

▲ Winter in the Pyrenees. The mountains of Gredos, Guadarrama and Sierra Nevada have similar skiing stations.

◄ A hotel goes up on the sand dunes. Hastily erected buildings are sometimes finished before the streets around them.

41

A tradition of craftsmanship

The versatile olive

▼ Beating olives out of the tree. This is the traditional method of collecting the fruit, which grows mostly in the south.

▼ Olive Oil is one of Spain's best-known products. It is used extensively for cooking and salad-making.

Traditional crafts

In a side street off Madrid's Gran Vía, a tinsmith hammers away, making beautiful lanterns and picture frames out of rolls of thin metal. He is the last of his family to have taken up the trade. When he retires the shop will probably close.

In an era of mass-produced merchandise *artesanos* find it difficult to make ends meet. But one can still find men and women who take pride in the handicrafts they learned from their parents.

Ceramics workers fare well, for much of their work goes to shops big and small. It is also sold at roadside stands and, of course, in the towns where it is made. Two of the most famous are Manises, near Valencia, which has produced quality ceramics since the eighteenth century, and Talavera de la Reina, in the Province of Toledo, whose wares feature charming folk designs. In La Mancha, the Don Quixote country, almost every village has its own *álfar* where the *alfarero* turns out rustic dinnerware and handsome pitchers for local use.

Lacemaking

Authentic bobbin lace is still made at Almagro, also in La Mancha, where women sit around the *plaza* pinning and unpinning the many threads needed for a design. This is edging or trimming lace, not to be confused with the netting in mantillas, virtually all of which is nowadays made by machine.

Embroidery and its sister art rugmaking also flourish throughout the country. Some of the prettiest bedspreads and rugs are woven in Murcia, where towns like Lorca and Mula employ many skilful weavers.

The art of sherry making

1. The harvested grapes are laid out to dry.

The sherry-manufacturing process begins with the drying of the grapes on esparto grass mats. When this is done, they are emptied in wooden troughs called *lagares* where men with hobnailed boots stamp on them to extract the juice (with labour costs rising, this may soon be done by machine). The liquid is then run into casks and put in *bodegas* or warehouses. Now called *mosto*, it ferments slowly for several months. When it becomes wine, it is put in new casks containing a quantity of spirit. There it will grow *flor*, the yeast-like ingredient that has great importance in sherrymaking, as it will determine the type of wine that emerges, i.e., *fino* (dry) or *oloroso* (full bodied). To assure uniform quality, sherry drawn out for shipment is substituted in the cask by the next younger wine; this in its turn is replaced by an even younger one—and so on on a rota system, allowing all supplies to age evenly.

3. The wine ferments for several months in the *bodega* or warehouse.

4. Casks are successively filled to ensure even ageing and uniform quality.

▲ Oranges are one of the country's main exports. They are grown in Valencia and shipped all over the world. Valencian farmers count their wealth in terms of orange trees and tend them with the best agricultural methods.

▼ Lace-making is one of Spain's most colourful crafts. This doll-seller in Majorca is wearing the handmade *mantilla* typical of that region. On the mainland Almagro, a little town in La Mancha, has been known for the quality of its lace since the Middle Ages.

2. Men wearing hobnailed boots stamp on the grapes in wooden troughs called *lagares*.

5. A technician adds colouring and sweetening to the dry sherry.

How a Spanish guitar is made

The guitar was originally an Andalusian and gypsy instrument. Today it is the basis of folk and pop music in many countries. Fine spanish guitars are still made by hand.

▲ The mould of the guitar. To give the instrument its "waist", a strip of wood is held to a hot tubular "bending iron".

▲ To prevent warping, the neck is made of laminated wood—walnut, maple or rosewood are preferred.

▲ Stringing the guitar. Strings are attached to the bridge at one end and the tuning pegs at the other.

▲ Strumming the guitar in rock or cowboy fashion. Hand and arm positions differ in classical playing.

Getting about in Spain

The Talgo express

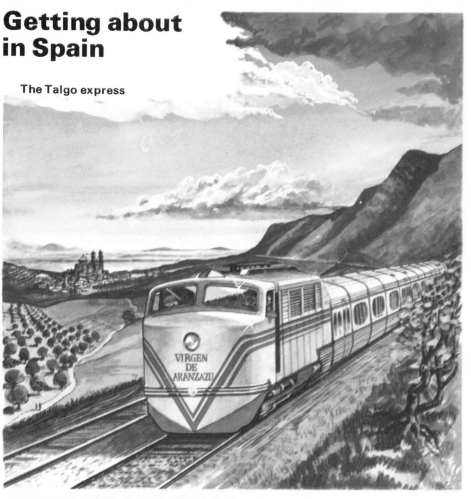

Cars and public transport

The most important public transport systems in Spain are to be found in Madrid and Barcelona. Both cities have an abundance of buses as well as a *metro* or underground. In the case of Barcelona, the tube service is complemented by a network of fast commuter trains.

Car ownership reached its peak during the economic boom of the sixties. But the rise in the number of private vehicles has complicated rather than helped the transport problem, for it has produced some of the continent's worst rush-hour traffic jams. What is more, since most Spaniards go home for lunch, the bottlenecks take place not just twice, but four times daily!

Railways in Spain

Cars are of course handiest for long-distance travel. At holiday time, families climb into their Spanish-made cars and head for the mountains or the seashore. For those who prefer trains there are the State Railways, or RENFE (*Red nacional de ferrocarriles españoles*). RENFE's equipment ranges from the very old to the modern high-speed trains known as TERs. Steam trains are still in use on local lines. Some have almost Victorian decor—right down to tasselled fringes. The fastest trains run at night, though even they are slow. The showpiece is still the *Talgo*, a silver, bullet-shaped train designed by Basque Engineer Alejandro Goiecoechea in 1930. The *Talgo* is still, today, surface transport at its finest.

▲ The Talgo, designed by Alejandro Goiecoechea, is low-slung, fast and ranks among Europe's most comfortable trains.

▼ The mule or horse-drawn *carreta* is still a feature on country roads.

▲ Buses in Madrid. Rush-hour jams here are among the worst in Europe.

44

Iberia—the national airline of Spain

Iberia Airlines began in 1921 as the *Compañía Española de Tráfico Aéreo,* a daily mail service between Andalucía and Morocco. Four years later came the *Union Aérea Española,* which offered international and domestic passenger service. Its successor, the *Compañía Aérea de Transporte,* became the direct ancestor of today's Iberia.

At present the company's fleet includes thirteen Caravelle 6Rs, six Caravelle 10Rs, three Boeing 747s, seven DC-8-53F, six DC-8-63s, two Boeing 727-200s, thirty-six DC-9-30s, plus two Fokker VFW F.28 Fellowships (for training) and eight Fokker VFW F.27 Friendship 200 turboprops.

▲ Exit from a toll motorway. There are also toll tunnels. These modern, multi-lane roads have eased cross-country traffic.

Madrid bus and metro tickets

▲ Madrid's transport system includes a cable car service between the busy Rosales Boulevard and the Casa de Campo park. The cable car escapes the crush at street level, and offers a fine view.

◀ Tickets for Madrid's buses and metro. The fare on a normal-sized bus is 5 pesetas. *Microbuses,* which are smaller and faster, charge 8 pesetas.

▼ A policeman directs traffic in Madrid's Calle de Alcalá. His force is separate from the armed police, or *policía armada.*

Heroes borrowed and lent

Characters from abroad

Folk heroes, both new and forgotten, have come to life recently in Spain thanks to the publishing boom and the impact of TV.

Some of these heroes come from abroad, as old *Robín de los bosques* (or "Robin of the Woods"). The Outlaw of Sherwood Forest, a favourite of generations past, has found his way back to Spain by way of a television serial.

Tales of another "outlaw", the formidable William created by Richmal Crompton in England, continue to sell steadily in book stores. *Guillermo*, as he is called in Spain, has been delighting Spanish children for over thirty years and shows no sign of losing his hold over bookworms who like to laugh as well as learn.

In the comic-book field a new figure from France, Astérix, has become immensely popular. Astérix even goes to school among the textbooks, to be read between classes or at recreation time.

Legends and Fiction

Meanwhile, the world is still enjoying the classical tales of three Spanish heroes. The greatest among them is undoubtedly Don Quixote, the comic knight-errant of the novel by Cervantes first published in 1605. This remarkable book has been translated into every Western language, filmed, set to music and choreographed.

Don Juan Tenorio, another Spanish folk figure, has also leapt abroad. Mozart wrote an opera about this unsavoury character, whose story was first set down by Tirso de Molina in 1630. Lord Byron, George Bernard Shaw and composer Richard Strauss were also inspired by the antics of the utter rotter from old Seville, and gave the world some memorable versions of them.

A completely different kind of hero was Rodrigo Díaz de Vivar, whose feats were the subject of a recent film. Rodrigo actually lived in the 11th Century and fought bravely against the Moors. The Muslims themselves so respected him that they gave him the title *Sidei* ("my lord"). His thrilling story, "The Song of My Cid", is the epic poem of the Spanish people.

El Cid—a soldier of honour

▼ The statue of El Cid in San Diego, California. He rides to battle on *Simpleton*, his loyal and far from simple horse.

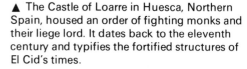

▲ The Castle of Loarre in Huesca, Northern Spain, housed an order of fighting monks and their liege lord. It dates back to the eleventh century and typifies the fortified structures of El Cid's times.

A French translation of Don Quixote

L'HISTOIRE
DE L'INGENIEVX,
ET REDOVTABLE
Cheualier,

DOM-QVICHOT
DE LA MANCHE.

Composée en Espagnol, Par Miguel de Ceruantes, Saauedra.
Et traduicte fidelement en nostre Langue,
Par F. DE ROSSET.

A PARIS,
Chez Iacqves dv Clov, & Denis
Morbav, rue S. Iacques, à la Salemandre.
M. DC. XVIII.
Auec Priuilege du Roy.

Don Quixote de la Mancha was a country gentleman who read too many tales of chivalry and daring. He proclaimed himself a champion of people in distress, donned a suit of armour and rode out in search of adventure. With his servant Sancho Panza pressed into service as "squire", the don found plenty to do.

► One day they came across a row of windmills on the crest of a hill. Don Quixote immediately declared them to be evil giants and hurled himself upon the sails. A gust of wind set them in motion. Up went Don Quixote, lance and all, to the dismay of the good Sancho, who, like most people, thought his master mad.

The adventures of Don Juan

The Don Juan legend tells of a dashing scoundrel who glorified in deceiving women and came to a terrible end.

◄ He had killed the father of one of his favourite ladies, Doña Ana de Ulloa. While Don Juan is walking past the grave one day, the statue of Comendador de Ulloa comes to life. The Don flippantly invites him to a banquet he is about to give. That night, the statue appears and terrifies the servants. Only Don Juan is cool and unafraid, for he has a code of honour of his own; he never refuses a dare. So when the statue asks him to dine at the church the following night, Don Juan readily agrees. The statue's meal consists of the hideous meats of the dead, but still Don Juan shows no fear. Then the statue asks him to give it his hand. Don Juan again accepts, but this is his downfall, for all the fires of hell flow from the hand.

Giants of art and thought

The Golden Age

In the centuries before the tourist boom, Spain was visited almost exclusively by art lovers. Devoid of gaudy hotels or night-clubs, she offered her guests the beauty of her architecture and painting, shared with scholars the treasures of her literature and philosophy.

These were the achievements of a nation in decline, for Spanish culture had blossomed as the Empire lay dying. The Golden Age of Spanish letters ran roughly from the late sixteenth century to the end of the seventeenth. It was a joyous era. Never before did the nation know such brilliance —or enjoy itself so thoroughly. Crowds packed theatres everywhere. On the bill were *comedias* by Felix Lope de Vega and Pedro Calderón de la Barca, poet-playwrights whose works are still unmatched today.

In painting, El Greco and Zurbarán gave Spain masterpieces which were to be prized by the whole world in centuries to come. Indeed, Spanish art was destined to become the foremost expression of the country's culture, with Velázquez and Goya as its chief representatives.

A great tradition

Realism was always the keynote in Spanish literature. The 1554 novel *Lazarillo de Tormes* describes in ghoulish detail the hideous tricks played by a boy on the tyrannical blind man he led. Cervantes, the master of all Spanish writers, was faithful to this tradition not only in *Don Quixote*, but in many other works. As late as the nineteenth century, the great novelist Pérez Galdós was working in this vein; his books treat the manners of that age with unusual compassion.

At the turn of that century came Spain's second great defeat—this time at the hands of the Americans in Cuba. In the shock that followed, a group of writers and thinkers sat down to the agonizing task of explaining the roots of Spain's decline. They came to be called *The Generation of* 1898. Among them were two giants of European philosophy—Miguel de Unamuno and José Ortega y Gasset.

▲ Goya's "Shootings of May 2nd" depicts the execution of Spanish guerrillas at the hands of the French in 1808. It is a high point in Spanish art—and one of the most bitter comments on man's brutality ever put on canvas. The Aragonese Francisco de Goya y Lucientes (1794–1828) brought a rough, unsparing realism to all his work, whether he was doing royal portraits or the likeness of men and women of the people. His etchings are masterpieces of the art, covering a variety of grim subjects from the daydreams of the insane to a collection entitled "The Disasters of War".

◀ Ignatius of Loyola was a red-headed Basque playboy, the scion of a rich and aristocratic family. He won fame on the battlefield, but a cannon ball shattered one of his legs in 1521. During his convalescence, Ignatius of Loyola began to page through the *Lives of the Saints*. He decided not only to enter the religious life, but to found an order of his own, the Society of Jesus. Unlike monks, Jesuits did not shun the world but mixed freely with people. They grew into one of the most important religious orders of the Catholic Church.

▲ Pablo Ruiz Picasso, born in Malaga in 1881, blazed not one but several trails in the art world of his day. He mastered half a dozen styles as his gift developed, pursuing his own, Picassian expression of the wonder of life. At his death in France in 1973 he was the acknowledged master of all that is vital and stimulating in modern art.

▲ "Women of Algiers", Picasso's version of a canvas by the nineteenth century artist Delacroix. The original is a portrait of three Arab girls; in Picasso's hands it has become a spinning-wheel of jagged surfaces and broken limbs. Nonsensical? Far from it. The scene has been carefully recomposed so that light and shadow, hues and textures assume different relations and (here is the point) produce a different emotional impact. Picasso's brush, like an ever-turning kaleidoscope, simply reassembles the shapes and colours of what the human eye calls "reality".

▼ Andrés Segovia, the world's best known guitarist. His repertoire ranges from Spanish classics of the Golden Age to the Baroque music of Germany and France and the work of modern masters. Segovia's playing is restrained and utterly lacking in "fireworks": in his hands the guitar is worthy of the noblest music.

◄ Eccentric Salvador Dali, famous for his surrealistic paintings of nightmares and fantasies. His grotesque but witty canvases in this style are only part of his output. Dali is equally celebrated as an illustrator. He has produced extraordinary drawings for *Don Quixote* and Dante's *Divine Comedy*. In the past Dali lived both in France and in America. He has returned to his native Catalonia, and now works in a magnificent villa on the Costa Brava.

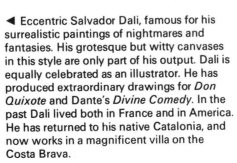

The Spanish character

Spanish honour

Contradiction is the hallmark of the Spanish character. The average Spaniard can be generous to a fault, but intolerant like few men on earth. He will take pride in calling himself an individualist while conforming to the standards of a closed society. He will do anything to save face, but risk everything —including prestige—in defence of a cause he deems worthy.

His generosity is staggering. It is born of a genuine concern for people combined with a superb disregard for material values. From childhood up he has been taught to share— and share he does, quite often putting himself out in order to help the friend or stranger who stands before him.

In sharp contrast to his material generosity is the meanness of his intellectual outlook. He has little or no tolerance of other people's views. He believes his moral standards are (or should be) universal, and deplores any deviation from them anywhere in the world.

Natural extremists

The Spaniard styles himself an individualist but conforms to medieval ethics and the dictates of a stern government. Though he may speak against them, the thought of actually tampering with traditional values and political authority fills him with dread —as well it might if he thinks of the country's bloody past. An extremist by nature, he knows no middle ground between blind obedience and blind destruction.

The Spaniard is supremely elegant, both in appearance and behaviour. He has a deeply seated urge to shine, or, in a tight situation, at least to *quedar bien* or come off honourably.

Best of all, the Spaniard can turn on his grisly but delightful humour to take the sting out of defeat. A foreign journalist once stumbled upon a village in the South whose inhabitants had made their livelihood from a local mill; now it was closed, they explained, they called it "the hunger factory".

▲ Self-improvement comes to naught. Debunking human aspirations has been a standard theme in Spanish humour since the time of Cervantes. The little man who loses his battle with the muscle developer is a direct descendant of Don Quixote.

▲ A chat after Mass. Women are especially pious; in small communities their lives revolve about the home and the Church. For years society frowned on women wage-earners.

But city girls are now finding jobs in offices and shops and a few even work after they marry. There are also more female university students.

Some characteristics of the Spanish

▲ The Spaniard's anger is very close to the surface of his skin. He reacts quickly and aggressively to any provocation.

▲ Few races are as generous with material things as the Spanish. Food is always shared, even with strangers.

▲ Tradition plays an important role in Spanish life. These young musicians have donned regional costume to perform at the Saffron Festival in Consuegra, a small town in La Mancha.

▼ A clergyman abandons his flock by walking on water: Spanish wit at its irreverent best. Whenever censorship permits, cartoonists and writers attack established values and even government policy.

▲ Schoolboys head for home and a succulent *merienda*. Their vitality springs from a secure family background in which ties are strong and long-lasting.

▲ Appearances are all-important in Spain. People wear the latest fashions, are judged on their clothes and bearing.

▲ A Spaniard is proud of being himself. He deeply resents becoming an object of idle curiosity or ridicule.

▲ Dignity is a mark of all social classes. On a personal level a Spaniard is seldom intimidated.

A nation on the move

Industrial development

In the last twenty years Spain has undergone a great change. From a country scarred by civil war it has become a nation humming with commerce and industry.

The economic boom brought many social changes. As factories sprang up, villagers flocked to them in search of work. One by one, little *pueblos* became ghost towns while the populations of metropolitan centres like Madrid and Barcelona grew. Modern flats were built to house the newcomers. Schools and hospitals were put up to serve their needs.

Other Spaniards sought work abroad. Thousands took factory jobs in France, Germany, Holland and Belgium. They return with savings and an intimate knowledge of life in developed, democratic countries quite unlike their own. Outwardly, at least, their homeland now bears a striking resemblance to these countries.

Political progress

Spain is changing rapidly in many ways, especially politically. Now that King Juan Carlos rules, government is more democratic and much more open. But from 1939 up till the death of Franco in 1975, political rule had been 'organic'. Spaniards had used this word to describe a system in which there was no legally-constituted Opposition. On the contrary, all legislators, civil servants and labour leaders were forced to show uncritical loyalty to Generalisimo Franco, then Head of State.

The majority of Spaniards are glad that their country has adopted a more open European system. But most Spanish people do not give a thought to politics. They think all forms of government are corrupt, and are content to enjoy the consumer goods and modern conveniences industrialization has brought.

▼ Communal pump. Most towns have running water, but bucketfuls are still drawn for laundry and other household purposes.

▲ Harvesting garlic. Modern machinery is now widely used in Spanish farming.

► A cellulose factory. Industrialization is changing the face of Spain.

▼ Irrigation has always been one of Spain's greatest problems. The Franco regime's first efforts towards industrialization began with the building of *pantanos* to conserve and distribute water. This dam is in Alarcon, in the Province of Cuenca, and forms a large man-made lake.

▲ Since Franco's death, the government has legalized trade unions, and strikes are no longer illegal.

▼ Old and new flats side by side in Alicante, on the Mediterranean Coast. These contrasts are common in Spain.

Finding work outside Spain

Switzerland
W. Germany
France
Other countries

in thousands of workers

115
110
100
90
80
70
60
50
40
30
20
10
0

1965 1966 1967 1968 1969 1970 1971 1972

▲ An acute shortage of work forces more than 100,000 Spaniards to migrate yearly. They take factory jobs abroad, in many cases leaving families behind.

▲ Abandoned houses in Andalucia. Villages and hamlets have become ghost towns as their inhabitants migrate to big cities.

Reference
Climate
Geography

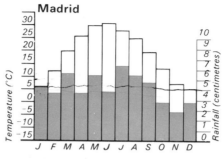

Madrid

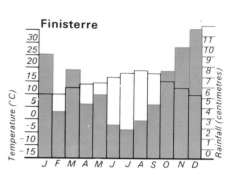

Finisterre

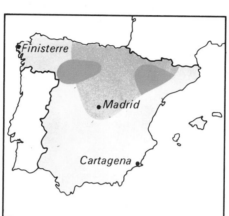

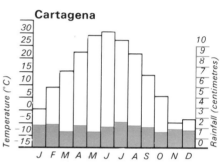

Cartagena

Land and people

Full title: Estado Español (Spanish State).

Position: 39 50N 3 40W in south-west Europe, occupying most of Iberian peninsula; Portugal lies to the west, and Gibraltar is a British enclave in the south.

Constituent parts: Continental Spain; Balearic Islands (Mallorca, Menorca, Ibiza, Formentera and several islets) which form a province; Canary Islands, divided into two provinces, Santa Cruz de Tenerife (Tenerife, Palma, Gomera, Hierro) and Las Palmas (Gran Canaria, Lanzarote, Fuerteventura, plus several barren islands); Ceuta and Melilla, enclaves on the Moroccan coast which are administered respectively as parts of Cadiz and Malaga provinces.

Area: 504,879 sq.km. (194,883 sq.m.)

Population: (1976) 36,161,000.

Capital: Madrid, pop. 4,344,379 (1975)

Language: Spanish; Catalan is also spoken in the north-east and Basque in the north; a minority speak Galician.

Religion: Catholicism is the established religion; about one per cent are protestants.

The State: The Spanish State was proclaimed on October 1, 1936, though its authority was complete only with the end of the Civil War on April 1, 1939.

Head of State: H.M. King Juan Carlos I.

Prime Minister: Adolfo Suarez

Political System: Parliamentary monarchy.

Armed Forces: Total 301,000; army 220,000; navy 47,500; airforce 33,500. The U.S. has air and naval bases in Spain.

International Organizations: Spain is a member of the United Nations, the Organization for Economic Cooperation and Development and the Council of Europe.

The natural vegetation of Spain

Forest Vegetation

Mixed Broad-leaved & Coniferous Woodland & Meadow

Mediterranean Evergreen Forest

Mediterranean Evergreen Maquis & Meadow

Mountain Forest

Grass Vegetation

Salt Steppe & Semi-Desert

Desert Vegetation

Alpine

South limit of Beech

North limit of Olive

The population density

Inhabitants

per mile²		per km²
under 32		under 12
32 - 64		12 - 25
64 - 128		25 - 50
128 - 256		50 - 100
256 - 512		100 - 200
over 512		over 200

● Cities with over 250,000 inhabitants

As is to be expected, the greatest densities of population are to be found around the main centres of industry and commerce: Bilbao, Zaragoza and Barcelona in the north; Madrid in the centre, and Valencia, Murcia, Málaga and Seville in the south. These urban areas have expanded fast over the last decade because of the rapid expansion of the Spanish economy. What is called a drift from the land in other countries is an understatement in Spain. People have left rural occupations and moved to the cities to 1972 this figure had dropped to a mere 14 per cent. Most of the people who deserted rural occupations have gone to the cities to seek their fortune, but many also have emigrated to Switzerland, France, Germany, or Britain where wages are much higher.

The population of principal towns

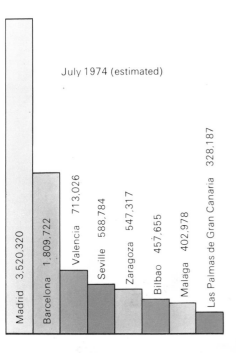

July 1974 (estimated)

Madrid 3,520,320
Barcelona 1,809,722
Valencia 713,026
Seville 588,784
Zaragoza 547,317
Bilbao 457,655
Malaga 402,978
Las Palmas de Gran Canaria 328,187

Government

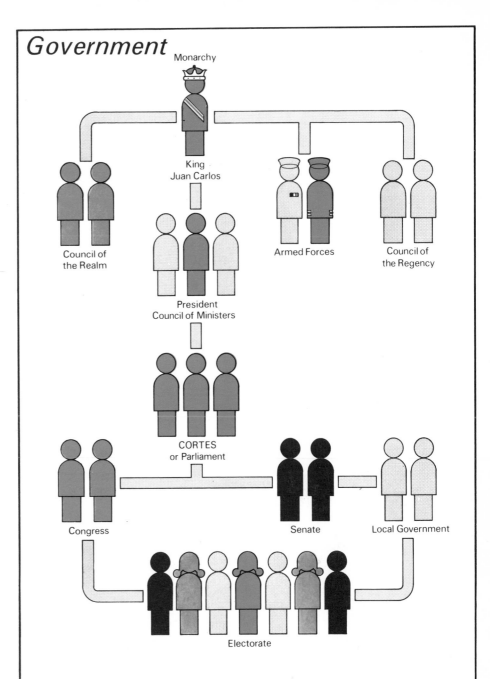

Monarchy

King Juan Carlos

Council of the Realm

Armed Forces

Council of the Regency

President Council of Ministers

CORTES or Parliament

Congress

Senate

Local Government

Electorate

Two days after the death of Generalisimo Franco, Prince Juan Carlos was sworn in as King of Spain, and the country entered a new era. The King appointed Rafael Arias Navarro as Premier and made ready to recast the nation's government along new, more democratic lines.

When Arias proved unsympathetic to some of his reforms, Juan Carlos dismissed him and in his place appointed Adolfo Suarez as Prime Minister. The Cortes was disbanded and in June, 1977, free elections were held for the new Parliament that took the Cortes' place. Premier Suarez's own party, the *Union de Centro Democratico*, came first among the many groups that took part in this election. Others took their places in the opposition: the Strong Spanish Socialist Workers' Party was joined in the Cortes by the Popular Socialist Party and the Spanish Communist Party on the left, the Popular Alliance on the right, and several other parties.

One of the new parliament's first tasks was the drafting, study and approval of a new Constitution. They also turned their attention to the demands for self-government among Spain's regions. Catalonia obtained self-government in 1977. The Basques were not far behind. Other regions seeking self-government are Andalucia, Extremadura and the Canary Islands.

Reference
History

Main events in Spanish history

B.C.
8th C.	Phoenicians found Cadiz
6th C.	Greeks, Carthaginians and last Celts arrive
206	Cadiz falls to Rome
151	Romans found Cordoba
19	Conquest by Rome complete

A.D.
409	Vandals, Alans and Suevi invade, ending Roman rule
414	Visigoths invade and are soon masters
589	Roman Catholicism state religion
711–18	Muslim conquest from North Africa
718	Christian reconquest begins
801	Charlemagne's son recaptures Barcelona from Muslims
1035	Sancho the Great of Navarre dies and Castile and Aragon become monarchies
1085	Alfonso VI recaptures Toledo from Muslims
1094	El Cid captures Valencia
1162	Aragon and Catalonia unite
1188	Towns first represented in Cortes
1230	Castile and Leon reunited
1238	Muslim kingdom of Granada emerges
1443	Naples taken by Alfonso V of Aragon
1469	Ferdinand of Aragon marries Isabella of Castile
1479	Castile and Aragon united under Ferdinand and Isabella
1516	Charles I, Hapsburg, succeeds to united kingdom of Castile and Aragon
1519	Ferdinand Magellan sets out from Seville on voyage round world
1519–22	Cortes conquers Mexico for Spain
1520–23	Internal revolts in Spain
1531–4	Pizarro conquers Peru for Spain
1554	Philip, Charles' son, marries Mary Tudor of England
1556–98	Philip II
1620	Spain enters Thirty Years' War
1640–59	Rebellion in Catalonia
1640	Portugal regains independence from Spain
1643	Major French victory over Spanish at Rocroi
1659	Peace of Pyrenees with France
1700	Charles II bequeathes Spain to Philip V, Louis XIV's grandson
1702–13	War of Spanish Succession
1704	Gibraltar lost to Britain
1713	Treaty of Utrecht: Spain loses Naples, Flanders and Milan
1767	Jesuits expelled
1805	French/Spanish fleet destroyed at Trafalgar by Nelson
1808	Napoleon puts brother Joseph on Spanish throne; Madrid *dos de mayo* rising against French leading to Peninsular War until 1814
1810–26	Spanish rule overthrown in mainland Spanish America
1812	Constitution of Cadiz: liberal and anti-clerical
1814	Ferdinand VII returns and tears up constitution
1820	Army enters politics for first time
1823	French army helps Ferdinand restore absolutism
1833–40	First Carlist war over succession between Isabella and Don Carlos
1846	'Spanish marriages' decided by France and Britain
1868	Isabella forced to abdicate
1872–6	Second Carlist war
1873–4	Republic declared; war in Cuba
1874	Alfonso XII, Isabella's son, enthroned
1898	Spanish-American war: Spain loses Philippines, Cuba, Puerto Rico
1912	Spanish protectorate in Morocco
1923–30	Captain-General of Catalonia, Primo de Rivera, dictator of Spain
1927	Rif revolt in Morocco under Abd el Krim finally crushed with French aid
1931	Alfonso XIII leaves Spain; Republic declared
1936–9	Civil War: Franco's Nationalists win
1947	Law of Succession: Franco to be succeeded by monarch
1955	Spain admitted to United Nations
1956	Morocco independent
1960	342 Basque priests protest at police brutality to political prisoners
1962	Asturias coal miners' strike begins wave of serious industrial action Franco announces succession to go to Prince Juan Carlos
1970	Basque separatists sentenced at Burgos to 30 years' imprisonment
1973	Luis Carrero Blanco made first Prime Minister; assassinated December

RULERS OF SPAIN
1479–1516	Ferdinand and Isabella (Ferdinand II of Aragon 1479–1516; Isabella I of Castile 1474–1504)
1516–56	Charles I (after 1519, Charles V of the Holy Roman Empire)
1556–98	Philip II
1598–1621	Philip III
1621–65	Philip IV
1665–1700	Charles II
1700–46	Philip V
1746–59	Ferdinand VI
1759–88	Charles III
1788–1808	Charles IV
1808–13	Joseph Bonaparte
1814–33	Ferdinand VII
1833–68	Isabella II
1871–3	Amadeo I
1873–4	First Spanish Republic
1875–85	Alfonso XII
1886–1931	Alfonso XIII (1923–30 Primo de Rivera dictator)
1931–9	Alcala Zamora
1936–9	President Manuel Azana
1936—	Generalisimo Francisco Franco Bahamonde

Ferdinand and Isabella: the Catholic Sovereigns
1474	Henry IV of Castile dies; his sister, Isabella, and her husband, Ferdinand, proclaimed Queen and King of Castile
1478	New Inquisition begins in Castile
1479	Ferdinand succeeds as King of Aragon; Isabella sends judicial commissions to put down noble lawlessness
1480	Lawyers begin to run Royal Council, taking over from nobles
1485	Inquisition starts in Aragon
1492	Capture of Granada completes Christian 'reconquest' of Muslim Spain; Jews told to become Christian; many flee; Isabella agrees to finance Columbus; he sails from Palos, reaches San Salvador in Bahamas, also Cuba and Hispaniola
1493–6	Columbus's second voyage: Lesser Antilles, Puerto Rico reached
1494	Spain and Portugal divide areas of discovery by Treaty of Tordesillas
1498–1500	Columbus's third voyage: Venezuela
1502	Muslims told to convert or leave; many convert and become Moriscos
1502–4	Columbus's fourth voyage: Honduras–Panama
1504	Ferdinand wins back whole of Naples from France
1512	Wins back Navarre from France

Philip II: Spain's zenith and decline
1555	Charles V abdicates. Low Countries go to Philip; he becomes King of Spain and Italian dependencies in 1556
1557	Philip fights Pope Paul IV
1559	Inquisition arrests head of Spanish church Treaty of Cateau-Cambresis ends French war
1560	Philip's naval force destroyed by Turks
1561	Philip makes Madrid capital
1563	Philip begins building of Escorial near Madrid—half-palace, half-monastry
1567	Muslim practices banned
1568–70	Morisco rising of Alpujarras cruelly put down; Moriscos deported from Granada and scattered throughout Spain
1571	Don Juan of Austria leads Spanish/Papal/Venetian victory over Turks at Lepanto
1576	'Spanish fury': Antwerp sacked by unpaid Spanish troops
1579	United Provinces (Low Countries) declare independence from Spain
1580	Philip incorporates Portugal into Spain

1584	Philip allies with Henry, Duke of Guise, head of Catholic League in France
1587	Drake's raids on Cadiz and Lisbon
1588	Defeat of Armada
1589	England intervenes to no avail in Portugal
1590	Spanish intervention in France begins
1595	Henry IV of France declares war on Spain
1596	Drake's raid on Cadiz destroys 65 ships
1598	(May) Peace of Vervins between France and Spain (Sept.) Philip dies

Republic and Civil War

1931	(Apr.) Municipal elections: great victory for Republicans; Alfonso XIII leaves (Dec.) Republican constitution adopted; Alcala Zamora President; Azana premier; radical reforms and proposals begin
1932	(Aug.) Military royalists under Gen. Sanjurjo revolt in Seville; suppressed (Sept.) Catalans force government to recognise their autonomy
1933	(Jan.) First of series of risings by anarcho-syndicalists, in Barcelona (Nov.) Right gain in Cortes elections Falange founded by Primo de Rivera's son
1934	(Oct.) Catalans declare independence; miners revolt in Asturias; both put down
1936	(Feb.) Popular Front win elections; Azana premier; brings back 1931 constitution (May) Azana president (July) Gens. Franco and Mola start civil war with revolt in Spanish Morocco; H.Q. established on mainland at Burgos (Oct.) Rebels make Franco Chief of State (Nov.) Siege of Madrid starts; government moves to Valencia; Germany and Italy recognize Franco's government (Dec.) Protocol signed in London for non-intervention by foreign powers in Spain
1937	(Feb.) Rebels take Malaga with Italian aid (Mar.) Loyalists rout Italians at Guadalajara (Apr.) Rebels destroy Guernica (May) Germans bombard Almeria (June) Rebels take Bilbao, Santander (Oct.) Rebels capture Gijon; government moves to Barcelona (Nov.) Franco begins naval blockade (Dec.) Loyalist offensive near Teruel
1938	(Dec.) Franco starts main offensive in Catalonia
1939	(Jan.) Franco captures Barcelona with Italian help (Feb.) Britain, France recognize Franco (Mar.) Madrid surrenders; war ends (Apr.) Spain joins Germany, Italy and Japan in Anti-Comintern Pact.

Artists and writers

ART

Sánchez Coello, Alonso (c. 1531–90): portrait painter of Philip II

El Greco (Domenikos Theotokopoulos) (1541–1614): visionary and mystical style; *Burial of Count Orgaz, View of Toledo,* and other masterpieces

Ribalta, Francisco (1555–1628): first Spanish painter to abandon Mannerism for Tenebrism; *The Last Supper, Christ Bearing His Cross*

Zurbarán, Francisco de (1598–1664): most restrained and purest artist of Spanish Baroque; *Immaculate Conception,* monastic themes

Velázquez, Diego Rodriguez de Silva y (1599–1660): most important 17th C. painter; forerunner of moderns; subjects ranged from religion to portraits of royalty and Pope Innocent X; finest and later works: *Rokeby Venus, The Maids of Honour, The Tapestry Weavers*

Murillo, Bartolomé Esteban (1618–82): more delicate and sentimental baroque style; religious paintings, *Boys Eating Melon*

Goya y Lucientes, Francisco José de (1746–1828): style revolutionized Spanish art; painted Charles IV's family and results of French invasion; *Caprices, Disasters of War, Majas*

Picasso, Pablo (1881–1973): leading modern artist; murals, etchings, sculptures; passed through blue, pink, black and cubist periods by 1914; settled in Paris; *Guernica, Metamorphoses,* etc

Gris, Juan (Jose Victoriano Gonzalez) (1887–1927): Cubist painter; worked in Paris

Miró, Joan (1893—): abstract paintings, murals, sculpture; *Harlequin Carnival, Dog Barking at the Moon;* worked in Paris for time

Dalí, Salvador (1904—): early work surrealist; lately tried to synthesize avant garde and traditional in historical paintings

Tapiés, Antonio (1923—): abstract and experimental painter with strong influence on all modern Spanish painting; *Three Stains on Grey Space*

LITERATURE

Poema del mio Cid: 12th C. epic about Rodrigo Diaz de Vívar, whose exploits against the Muslims earned him the title Cid (*sidi* in Arabic means 'lord')

Cervantes Saavedra, Miguel de (1547–1616): novelist; *Don Quixote* is the brilliant forerunner of the modern novel

Góngora y Argote, Luis de (1561–1627): poet; dominated 17th C. Spanish poetry; developed *gongorismo* style; works include *Solitudes, Fable of Polyphemus and Galatea*

Lope de Vega, Felix (1562–1635): did for drama in Golden Age what Cervantes did for novel; prolific output includes *Perinãñez, Fuenteovejuna, No Judge like the King* (novels), *The Gardener's Dog* and other cloak-and-sword comedies

Tirso de Molina (pseud. of Gabriel Téllez) (1580–1648): important Golden Age dramatist; *The Seville Deceiver* is the first Don Juan story

Ruiz de Alarcón y Mendoza, Juan (1581–1634): outstanding dramatist of Golden Age; wrote only 20 plays, incl. satire *The Suspicious Truth,* imitated by Corneille

Calderón de la Barca, Pedro (1600–81): last of great dramatists and best-known outside Spain; his most characteristic plays capture mood of Spain in decline; *Life is a Dream, The Prodigious Magician, The Mayor of Zalamea, autos sacramentales* (morality plays)

Saavedra, Angel de (1791–1865): poet and dramatist; helped start Romantic movement in Spain; his play *Don Alvaro* used by Verdi as libretto for opera, *Force of Destiny*

Pérez Galdos, Benito (1843–1920): novelist: first Spanish writer of international stature for two centuries; *National Episodes* (46 vols.) and *Contemporary Novels* (over 30 vols.) captured life of 19th C. Spain

Unamuno, Miguel de (1864–1936): Basque poet, novelist, essayist, philosopher

Benavente, Jacinto (1866–1954): dramatist; master of social satire; Nobel Prize 1922

Pérez de Ayala, Ramón (1880–1962): novelist, essayist, poet; last novels, especially *Belarmino and Apolonio,* most significant

Jimenez, Juan Ramon (1881–1959): poet, a master of the short lyric; author of children's classic in poetic prose *Platero and I;* Nobel Prize 1956.

Ortega y Gasset, José (1883–1955): philosopher and essayist. *Invertebrate Spain, The Revolt of the Masses, The Modern Theme* all tried to trace patterns in history

Garcia Lorca, Federico (1898–1936): promising dramatist and established poet shot by Nationalists in Civil War. *Romancero Gitano, Poeta en Nueva York, Yerma*

Aleixandre, Vicente (1898–): poet, one of the leading figures of the "1927 Generation". *Sombra del paraiso.* Nobel Prize 1977.

Cernuda, Luis (1902–63): exiled poet, influential with younger poets.

57

Reference
The Economy

Agriculture in Spain

Sugar-beet   Olives   Cows

Rice   Principal Fishing Ports   Sheep

Rapid economic growth

The Spanish economy is booming. After a
very disappointing year in 1971, the economy
grew at 7.5 per cent in 1972 (compared with
Britain's 1–2 per cent). The main reasons for
this have been (a) the increase in earnings
from tourism and the money sent back home
by Spanish workers abroad; (b) the cutback
in imports; and (c) the big rise in exports of
industrial goods. The healthy state of the
economy is shown by the large surplus in
balance of payments (the credit/debit
account of dealings with other countries and
international bodies), and by the growth in
reserves of gold and foreign currencies to over
5,000 million ptas. by the end of 1972.

All these figures are very impressive. But
Spain has for a long time lagged behind in
Europe, and it needs to expand faster to close
the gap. In fact, the Spanish economy should
be growing much faster. The balance-of-
payments and reserve positions are really too
good, because they mean that resources are
being left unused.

Spain's industry is helped by tariff
protection, by low taxes, and by strict control
of workers, whose hours are longer than
anywhere else in Europe.

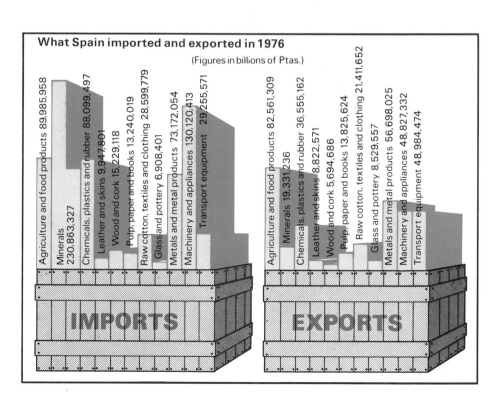

What Spain imported and exported in 1976

(Figures in billions of Ptas.)

IMPORTS
- Agriculture and food products 89,985,958
- Minerals 230,863,327
- Chemicals, plastics and rubber 88,099,497
- Leather and skins 9,947,801
- Wood and cork 15,229,118
- Pulp, paper and books 13,240,019
- Raw cotton, textiles and clothing 28,599,779
- Glass and pottery 6,908,401
- Metals and metal products 73,172,054
- Machinery and appliances 130,120,413
- Transport equipment 29,255,571

EXPORTS
- Agriculture and food products 82,561,309
- Minerals 19,331,236
- Chemicals, plastics and rubber 36,555,162
- Leather and skins 8,822,571
- Wood and cork 5,694,686
- Pulp, paper and books 13,825,624
- Raw cotton, textiles and clothing 21,411,652
- Glass and pottery 8,529,557
- Metals and metal products 56,698,025
- Machinery and appliances 48,827,332
- Transport equipment 48,984,474

Where Spaniards work

Services 35%

Construction 38%

Agriculture 26·5%

As Spain's economy grows rapidly, so more and more people are needed in industry and services. People leave farming and the countryside for better-paid factory and service jobs in the towns. Many go to Switzerland, Germany and France for even higher wages.

Industry in Spain

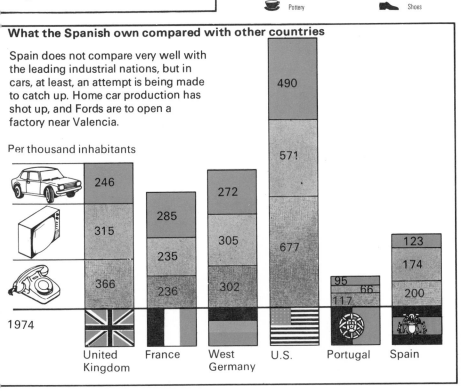

🏭	Major Industrial Centres	🍷	Glass	🛢	Beer	
⚙	Mechanical Engineering		Cement	✕	Weaponry	Lignite
🚗	Automobiles		Paper	🚚	Locomotives	
🚢	Shipbuilding		Tobacco Manufacturing	🏍	Motorcycles	◇ Principal Coalmining Areas
◎	Tyres		Sugar Refineries	🏭	Oil Refineries	
⚡	Electronics	✽	Leather	■	Iron-metallurgy	Textile Districts
☕	Pottery	👞	Shoes	▲	Chemicals	

What the Spanish own compared with other countries

Spain does not compare very well with the leading industrial nations, but in cars, at least, an attempt is being made to catch up. Home car production has shot up, and Fords are to open a factory near Valencia.

Per thousand inhabitants

1974

	United Kingdom	France	West Germany	U.S.	Portugal	Spain
Cars	246	285	272	490	95	123
TV	315	235	305	571	66	174
Telephones	366	236	302	677	117	200

How prices and incomes have risen

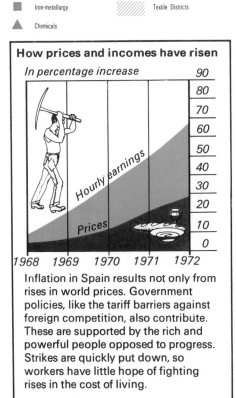

In percentage increase

Hourly earnings

Prices

1968 1969 1970 1971 1972

90 80 70 60 50 40 30 20 10 0

Inflation in Spain results not only from rises in world prices. Government policies, like the tariff barriers against foreign competition, also contribute. These are supported by the rich and powerful people opposed to progress. Strikes are quickly put down, so workers have little hope of fighting rises in the cost of living.

Gazetteer

Alicante. 38 22N 1 28W. Seaport and capital of Alicante province. Founded by Carthaginians in 3rd C. B.C. Exports wine, fruit, olive oil. Pop. 153,742.

Almería. 36 53N 2 33W. Seaport and capital of Almería province. Moorish stronghold 8th-15th C. Gothic cathedral. Exports grapes, minerals. Pop. 99,653.

Andalucía. 37. 20N 5 0W. Region and former province. Settled by Phoenicians in 11th C. B.C. Moorish state 8th-15th C., with monuments in Granada, Seville, Cordoba, etc. Very fertile land with olives, vine, fruit and cereals.

Aragón. 41 40N 0 40W. Region in N.E., formerly kingdom. United with Castile in 15th C. Sparsely populated. Main town Zaragoza.

Asturias. 43 20N 5 50E. Region in N.W. (identical with Oviedo province). Christian stronghold during Moorish rule south of the Cantabrian mountains which divide the region from the rest of Spain. Richest coal-mines in Spain.

Balearic Islands. 39 40N 3 0E. Archipelago in Mediterranean forming province. Four large islands: Majorca (Mallorca), Minorca (Menorca), Iviza (Ibiza), Formentera; and several islets. Tourism has taken over from vines, olives and almonds as main source of income. Succession of rulers before Moors and then Aragon from 1349. Capital Palma.

Barcelona. 41 24N 2 9E. Capital of Barcelona province. Chief seaport and industrial and commercial centre. 2nd largest city. Founded by Carthaginians under Hamilcar Barca. Part of Aragon after 1137. Cathedral, palace, churches, university (1430). Centre of Catalan culture and separatism, and of left-wing activists. Seat of Republican government in Civil War. Exports textiles, machinery, wine, olive oil, etc. Pop. 1,759,148.

Basque Provinces. 43 20N 2 20W. Region in N.E. comprising Alava, Guipúzcoa and Vizcaya. Basque is unrelated to any other language. Main city Bilbao.

Bilbao. 43 16N 2 53W. Capital of Vizcaya province. Important seaport. Iron and steel industry. Seat of Basque government in Civil War. Pop. 406,200.

Burgos. 42 21N 3 40W. Capital of Burgos province. Birthplace of El Cid, whose grave is in magnificent Gothic cathedral. Franco's capital in Civil War. Pop. 100,413.

Cadíz. 36 33N 6 20W. Capital of Cadíz province. Important seaport. Founded by Phoenicians c.1000 B.C. Columbus started second voyage; Drake burned Spanish fleet here 1587. Two cathedrals. Exports wine, olive oil, cork. Pop. 133,114.

Canary Islands. 28 0N 16 0W. Group in Atlantic off N.W. coast of Africa. Form two provinces: Las Palmas (Gran Canaria, Fuerteventura, Lanzarote) and Santa Cruz de Tenerife (Tenerife, Palma, Gomera, Hierro). Volcanic origin. People of Berber origin (Guanches). Tourism, fishing, canning important. Spanish since 1476. Capitals Las Palmas, Santa Cruz de Tenerife.

Cantabrian Mountains. 43 12N 5 20W. Range in N. along Bay of Biscay forming barrier from rest of Spain. Highest peak Peña Corredo (2,680 metres [8,794 ft.]). Rich in coal and iron.

Castile. Old Castile (41 30N 3 40W) and New Castile (40 0N 3 20W) make up eleven provinces. Former kingdom. United with León 1230, with Aragon 1479. Mainly infertile plateau.

Cataluña (Catalonia). 41 40N 1 30E. Region in N.E. forming four provinces. Own language (related to Provençal); own government 1932-9. Rich in agriculture; also most highly industrialized region in Spain.

Córdoba (Cordova). 37 54N 4 48W. Capital of Córdoba province. Typical Moorish town, with mosque (now cathedral) and distinctive architecture. Capital of Moorish Spain from 756. Conquered by Castile 1236. Industrial, commercial and tourist centre. Pop. 231,641.

Costa del Sol. 36 46N 4 47W. Coastline of S. from Almería to Tarifa. Tourist centres, e.g. Málaga, Torremolinos.

Costa Brava. 41 28N 2 30E. Coastline N. of Barcelona. Tourist centres, e.g. Tossa.

Ebro River. 41 0N 0 30E. In N.E. Rises in Cantabrian Mountains and flows 570 miles to Mediterranean. Ancient Iberus. Used with many tributaries for hydroelectric power.

Galicia. 42 45N 8 0W. Region and former kingdom in N.W. now forming four provinces. Cattle, pigs, maize, sardines. Main town La Coruna.

Granada. 37 17N 3 37W. Capital of Granada province. For 791 years centre of Moorish civilization until finally retaken by Christians in 1492. Alhambra palace finest piece of Moorish art in Spain. Also Generalife palace, Alacazaba castle, cathedral (with tomb of Ferdinand and Isabella). Pop. 163,912.

Guadalaqivir. River. 36 45N 6 25W. In S. Flows 360 miles through Andalucia to Seville and Atlantic. Name from Arabic *Wadi el-Kebir* ('Great River'). Used for irrigation.

Ibiza. See Balearic Islands.

Jerez. 36 42N 6 10W. Town in Cadiz province. Renowned for sherry. Pop. 145,574.

Las Palmas. 28 0N 15 45W. Capital of Las Palmas province of Canary Islands on Gran Canaria. Popular resort. Fruit, wine exports. Pop. 263,000.

León. 42 35N 5 35W. Region and former kingdom; covers five provinces including León province; united with Castile 1230. Capital of province is León.

Madrid. 40 27N 3 42W. Capital of Spain and Madrid province, and largest city. Taken from Moors 1083 by Castile. Capital since 1561 (except for 1601-6 when Valladolid). Besieged by Nationalists 1936-9 in Civil War. Roughly at Spain's geographical centre, on tableland 2,200 ft. up; hot summers and cold winters. Prado Museum has one of world's best art collections.

Communications and industrial centre. Pop. 3,100,000.

Majorca. See Balearic Islands.

Málaga. 36 46N 4 47W. Capital of Málaga province. Seaport, industrial and tourist centre (Costa del Sol). Founded by Phoenicians, occupied by Moors for 776 years and captured by Ferdinand and Isabella 1487. Pop. 350,977.

Minorca. See Balearic Islands.

Murcia. 38 0N 1 8W. Region and former kingdom (covering Murcia and Albacet provinces), province and town. Kingdom annexed to Castile 1269. Town important for textiles, especially silk, which dates from Moorish times. Cathedral. Pop. 261,960.

Navarra. 43 0N 1 45W. One of Basque provinces which once formed kingdom with Basses-Pyrenees department in France. Ferdinand annexed Spanish part in 1515. Capital Pamplona

Palma (de Mallorca). 39 37N 2 40E. Capital of Majorca and Balearic Is. Remains of Moorish castle, Gothic cathedral. Tourism, export of fruit. Pop. 199, 032.

Pyrenees (Pirineos). 42 30N 1 0E. Mountain range separating Spain and France. Highest peak Pico de Aneto 3,404 metres (11,168 ft.).

Seville. 37 27N 5 58W. Capital of Seville province and chief city of Andalucia. Major port and industrial centre on Guadalaqivir River. Ancient Hispalis. Captured by Romans 45 B.C., thrived under Moors till 1248. Gothic cathedral has tomb of Columbus. Birthplace of Velázquez and Murillo. Fourth largest city in Spain. Pop. 622,148.

Sierra de Guadarrama. 40 55N 3 50W. Mountain range N. of Madrid. Reaches 8,100 ft. in Peñalara. Timber and winter sport industries.

Tajo River (Tagus). 40 40N 2 12W. Flows 570 miles from E. Spain to Atlantic at Lisbon.

Tenerife. See Canary Is.

Toledo. 39 55N 4 0W. Capital of Toledo province, on Tajo River gorge. Long famed for swords; also firearms, textiles. Historic city. Capital of Visigothic Spain 569-711 and of Catholic Spain 1085-1561. Magnificent cathedral, houses paintings by El Greco, Goya, Rubens. Archbishop is primate of Spain. Pop. 41,000.

Valencia. 39 28N 0 23W. Region and former kingdom, province and Spain's third largest city. Kingdom covered three provinces, including Valencia province, and was Moorish emirate captured by El Cid, though kept separate identity till 18th C. City is port, industrial, commercial and tourist centre. Medieval cathedral; silk-market, university. Magnificent art collection. Pop. 624,227.

Valladolid. 41 40N 4 45W. Capital of Valladolid province. Industrial centre and railway junction. Cathedral, 13th C. university. Home of Cervantes, Columbus. Pop. 193,214.

Zaragoza (Saragossa). 41 38N 0 50W. Capital of Zaragoza province. Name derived from Caesarea Augusta. Roman walls preserved. Capital of Aragón 12th-15th C. Two cathedrals, castle, etc. Industrial centre and railway junction. Pop. 439,451.

Index

Numbers in heavy type refer to illustrations

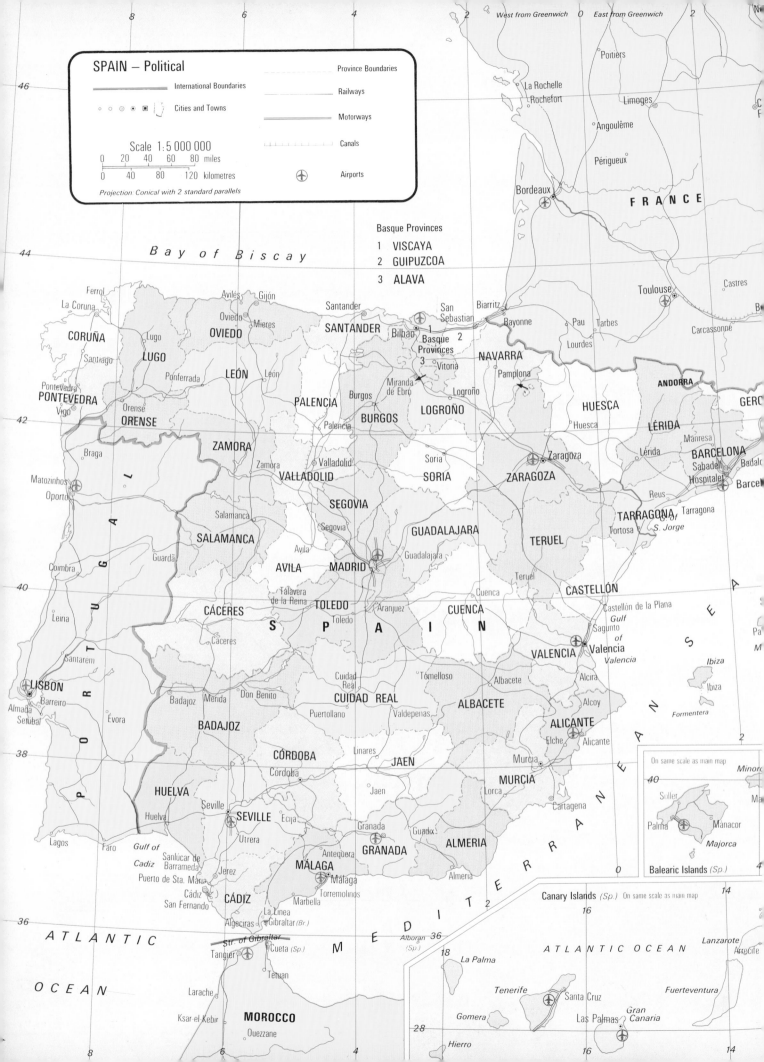

SPAIN – Political

International Boundaries	Province Boundaries
Cities and Towns	Railways
	Motorways
	Canals
Scale 1:5 000 000	Airports

0 20 40 60 80 miles
0 40 80 120 kilometres

Projection: Conical with 2 standard parallels

Basque Provinces
1 VISCAYA
2 GUIPUZCOA
3 ALAVA

West from Greenwich 0 East from Greenwich

Poitiers

La Rochelle
Rochefort

Limoges

Angoulême

Périgueux

Bordeaux

FRANCE

Toulouse

Castres

Bay of Biscay

Ferrol
La Coruña
Avilés Gijón
Santander
San Biarritz
Sebastian
Bayonne
Pau Tarbes

CORUÑA
Lugo
Oviedo Mieres
OVIEDO
SANTANDER
Bilbao 1 Basque 2
Provinces
3 Vitoria
Lourdes

Santiago
LUGO
Ponferrada
LEÓN
León
PALENCIA
Burgos
Miranda
de Ebro Logroño Pamplona
NAVARRA

ANDORRA

Pontevedra
PONTEVEDRA
Vigo
ORENSE
Orense
Braga
ZAMORA
Palencia
BURGOS
LOGROÑO
HUESCA
Huesca
LÉRIDA
Manresa
GERO

Matozinhos
Oporto
Zamora
Valladolid
Soria
Zaragoza
ZARAGOZA
Lérida
BARCELONA
Sabadell
Hospitalet
Barce

ZAMORA
VALLADOLID
SORIA
Reus
TARRAGONA
Tarragona
S. Jorge

Coimbra
Guarda
Salamanca
SEGOVIA
Segovia
Ávila
SALAMANCA
GUADALAJARA
TERUEL
Tortosa
Gulf
of

Leiria
Santarém
CÁCERES
Cáceres
Talavera
de la Reina
AVILA
MADRID
MADRID
Guadalajara
Aranjuez
Teruel
Cuenca
CASTELLÓN
Castellón de la Plana
Sagunto

S P A I N
TOLEDO
Toledo
CUENCA
VALENCIA
Valencia
Valencia
Ibiza

LISBON
Barreiro
Badajoz
Mérida
Don Benito
CUIDAD REAL
Cuidad
Real
Tomelloso
Albacete
Alcira
Ibiza

Almada
Setúbal
Évora
BADAJOZ
Puertollano
Valdepeñas
ALBACETE
Alcoy
Formentera

P O R T U G A L
Linares
CÓRDOBA
Córdoba
JAEN
MURCIA
Murcia
ALICANTE
Elche Alicante

HUELVA
Seville
Jaen
Lorca
MURCIA
Cartagena

Lagos
Faro
Gulf of
Cadiz
Sanlúcar de
Barrameda
SEVILLE
Utrera
Ecija
Antequera
Granada
Guadix
ALMERIA
Soller
Minor
40
Manacor
Balearic Islands (Sp.)

Puerto de Sta. María
Jerez
GRANADA
Palma
Majorca

Cádiz
San Fernando
CÁDIZ
MÁLAGA
Málaga
Torremolinos
Almería

La Línea
Marbella
Algeciras Gibraltar (Br.)
Str. of Gibraltar
Ceuta (Sp.)
Tangier
Alborán
(Sp.) **36**
Canary Islands (Sp.) On same scale as main map
14

A T L A N T I C
M E D I T E R R A N E A N   S E A

Tetuan
18
La Palma
A T L A N T I C   O C E A N
Lanzarote
Arrecife

O C E A N
Larache
Tenerife Santa Cruz
Fuerteventura

MOROCCO
Ksar-el-Kebir
Ouezzane
28
Gomera
Las Palmas
Gran
Canaria

Hierro
16
14

SPAIN – Physical

International Boundaries
Cities and Towns
8504 ▲ Mountain Peaks
Scale 1:5 000 000

| 0 | 20 | 40 | 60 | 80 | miles |

| 0 | 40 | 80 | 120 | kilometres |

Projection: Conical with 2 standard parallels

feet	metres
9000	2743
6000	1829
3000	914
1000	366
500	183
sea level	0

West from Greenwich 0 East from Greenwich

Nevers
Poitiers
Vienne
Vichy
Ile de Ré
La Rochelle
Rochefort
Limoges
Clermont
Ferrand
Puy de Dôme 4806
Ile d'Oleron
Angoulême
Mt. Dore 6190
Mt. du Cantal 6095
Massif
Périgueux
Médoc
Gironde
FRANCE
Central
Bordeaux
Dordogne
Lot
44
Garonne
Landes
GASCONY
Adour
Toulouse
Castres

Bay of Biscay

C. Ortegal
C. de Peña
Ferrol
Avilés
Gijón
La Coruña
Oviedo
Mieres
Santander
San Sebastian
Biarritz
Bayonne
Pau
Tarbes
Béziers
Narbon
Lugo
ASTURIAS
Picos de ▲8688
Cantabrian Mts
Bilbao
BASQUE
PROVINCES
Lourdes
Mt. Perdido 10,997
Pyrenees
Carcassonné
Perpignon
Santiago
GALICIA
Ponferrada
León
Ebro
Vitoria
Pamplona
Canfranc Pass 5350
P. de Aneto 11,168
ANDORRA
Pontevedra
Orense
Sil
Miranda de Ebro
NAVARRA
Logroño
Huesca
CATALONIA
Gerona
Vigo
Braga
Lima
Zamora
Campos
Palencia
Sierra de la Demanda
Aragon
Zaragoza
ARAGON
Lérida
Manresa
Sabadell
Badalona
Hospitalet
Barcelona
Oporto
Douro
OLD CASTILE
Valladolid
Duero
Soria
Ebro
Reus
Costa Brava
Coimbra
PORTUGAL
Salamanca
Tormes
Sierra de Guadarrama
Segovia
Peñalara 8100
Henares
Tortosa
G. of S. Jorge
C. de Tortosa
Guardã
Sa. de Gata
Avila
Guadalajara
Serrania de Cuenca
Teruel
Sierra de Gudur
VALENCIA
Suller
MADRID
Cuenca
Castellón de la Plana
Gulf of Saguntorn
Palma
Majorca
Leiria
Pico de Almanzor ▲ 8504
Sierra de Gredos
Talavera de la Reina
Tagus
Sa. Martés
Saguntó
Valencia
Ibiza
Cabrera
Santarem
Cáceres
SPAIN
Toledo
Aranjuez
NEW CASTILE
Tagus
Valencia
Ibiza
LISBON
Sa. de S. Pedro
Montes de Toledo
La Tomelloso
Júcar
Alcira
Tejo
EXTREMADURA
Guadiana
Cuidad Real
Mancha
Albacete
Alcoy
C. Nao
Barreiro
Badajoz
Mérida
Don Benito
Guadiana
Puertollano
Valdepeñas
Sa. de Alcaraz
MURCIA
Alicante
Costa Blanca
Évora
Sierra Morena
Linares
Sa. de Espuña
Elche
Murcia
Sa. de Aracana
Córdoba
La Sagra 7815
Sa. de Espuña
Lorca
Sangonera
C. de Palos
Cartagena
Sa. do Malhão
ANDALUSIA
Jaén
Segura
ALGARVE
Seville
Guadalquivir
Ecija
Granada
Guadix
Sa. de los Filabres
Lagos
Faro
Utrera
Sierra Nevada
Mulhacén 11421
Almería
C. de Gata
Huelva
Antequera
Gulf of Cadiz
Sanlúcar de Barrameda
Jerez
Málaga
Costa de la Luz
Puerto de Sta. Maria
Guadalete
Torremolinos
Cádiz
San Fernando
Marbella
Costa del Sol
La Linea
Gibraltar (Br.)
Algeciras
Europa Pt.
C. Trafalgar
C. Spatel
of Gibraltar
Tangier
Ceuta (Sp.)
MEDITERRANEAN SEA
Alboran (Sp.)
36
MOROCCO
Er Rif
Larache
Ksar el Kebir
Quezzane
Tetuan
ATLANTIC OCEAN

On same scale as main map
40
Suller
Minorca
Mahon
Palma
Manacor
Majorca
Balearic Islands (Sp.)

Canary Islands (Sp.) On same scale as main map
16
La Palma
Lanzarote
Arrecife
Tenerife
Santa Cruz
Gomera
Pico de Teide
Las Palmas
Gran Canaria
Fuerteventura
Hierro
28